LOST
MOHAWK
VALLEY

Bob Cudmore

LOST
MOHAWK
VALLEY

BOB CUDMORE

THE
History
PRESS

Published by The History Press
Charleston, SC 29403
www.historypress.net

Copyright © 2015 by Bob Cudmore
All rights reserved

First published 2015

Manufactured in the United States

ISBN 978.1.46711.838.5

Library of Congress Control Number: 2015945694

Notice: The information in this book is true and complete to the best of our knowledge. It is offered without guarantee on the part of the author or The History Press. The author and The History Press disclaim all liability in connection with the use of this book.

In memory of Vera Cudmore: "And if you get into trouble, name it after me."

CONTENTS

CONTENTS

PREFACE

In the preface to my last book was the story of Frances Burnham of Glenville. She provided clippings and photos about her great uncle, aviation pioneer Edward Pauley of Gloversville, as we sat at her dining room table. The story of Pauley's remarkable life and his death in a plane crash was told in the *Hidden History of the Mohawk Valley* chapter "Death Rode on the Wings of the Wind."

Frances Burnham died on September 23, 2013, just before *Hidden History* was published. Harold, her husband for fifty-seven years, told me she was eagerly awaiting the book version of her story that already existed in a photocopy form she had distributed to her extended family. Frances spent many hours researching family history. She was a role model for all of us on how to preserve the past.

ACKNOWLEDGEMENTS

Jerry Snyder, president of the Historic Amsterdam League, spent many hours working on the photos used in this book. Thanks also to Kathy Snyder, Jerry's wife, who was the photographer on several photo shoots. Former Montgomery County historian Jacqueline Murphy has been a constant supporter and has assisted with research, as has historian Christopher Philippo of Glenmont and David Fiske of Ballston Spa. Ann Peconie of the Walter Elwood Museum provided many pictures and insights for the chapter on milltown culture. Thanks to Montgomery County historian Kelly Farquhar, former Fulton County historian Peter Betz, Amsterdam city historian Robert von Hasseln, Bookhound proprietor Dan Weaver, World War II historian Robert N. Going and many more. My gratitude goes out to Old Peddler's Wagon proprietors Ed DiScenza and Ellen Benanto in Amsterdam for their retail support of my books.

Thank you to John Cropley, who edits my columns for the *Daily Gazette*. Audrey Sears provides encouragement and stimulating questions as research starts to uncover history stories. And thanks to you for buying and reading my books.

AUNT VERA

This book is dedicated to one of my aunts, Vera Cudmore, the first of our family born in America. Her parents, brothers and sisters, including my father, were all born in England.

ACKNOWLEDGEMENTS

In some ways, her life could be defined negatively. Vera never married and never owned a home but lived in several apartments in Amsterdam, choosing locations near where she worked. She never owned nor drove a car and always walked to work, for a long time in the shipping room at Fownes Brothers glove mill and later in the kitchen at St. Mary's Hospital.

She never embraced positive thinking. She was always sure the worst was about to happen. She never got the hang of the cordless phone that was supposed to help her answer calls when she was in the bathroom. She never caught on to computers.

She knew how to make friends. She had circles of friends, ranging from former cronies at Amsterdam's Ivy Leaf Tavern to devout members of the Sisters of St. Joseph of Carondelet. She was beloved for her common sense, good nature and humor. She was a wiz at word puzzles, wrote witty poems, sang funny songs and could recite the alphabet backward.

During her last twenty years, Vera lived alone in a series of three apartments at the Amsterdam Housing Authority high-rise for the elderly on Wall Street. She contributed mightily to the social scene in that building. She traveled on many bus trips and also made a memorable journey by airplane to California with her best friend, Sister Mary Englebert Lucha.

She never wanted to be on welfare and only went on Medicaid at the very end because she needed to be at a nursing home for a couple months.

Vera traveled light the last few years, sloughing off her belongings because she did not want to leave a lot of stuff behind for relatives to deal with. Still, she was eighty-five and had collected an eclectic set of household items.

Her photo array was politically correct, as far as the family was concerned. Each nephew and niece had photos displayed, along with other family members, plus pictures of Sister Englebert.

The day after Vera's funeral in 2002, her friend Don Macvean came from Vera's church, United Methodist, to take items for the church tag sale, providentially scheduled that weekend. It was both welcome and sad to see chairs, rugs, bookcases, clothing and lamps fly out of the apartment over the space of an hour or two. What had been Vera's place quickly became a few rooms with some pieces of furniture.

Rooting through what remained in her apartment, I came across things that took me back in time and made me smile. There were baskets she made out of old Christmas cards that are tied together with yarn. I still have one on my desk that holds my wallet and keys. There was paperwork from her umpteen years as treasurer of VFW Post 55 Auxiliary. There were plastic containers where she stored cookies and Pringles potato chips to fend off

ACKNOWLEDGEMENTS

insomnia, if her customary remedy of reading murder mysteries didn't send her to sleep.

She always complained about the sex and violence in the mystery books she borrowed from the Amsterdam Free Library. However, she complained in great detail, if you know what I mean.

One thing I saved for myself from Vera's apartment was the glass sugar container with the screw top, the classic kind, stolen by my son from his college dining hall and proudly used by Vera all these years. Vera was a frequent co-conspirator with the plans and schemes of people many years her junior.

When you asked Vera how she was feeling, she always said, "Rotten."

"I've got to go, Aunt Vera."

"Go on and have a good time. Enjoy yourself when you're young. Don't ever get old. Stay out of trouble. And if you get into trouble, name it after me."

Part I

A LOST WAY OF LIFE

CARPET MILL CULTURE
IN AMSTERDAM

On the Road for Mohawk,
Mill Girls and More

It was a rough Atlantic crossing for James Kindon, an English weaver who sailed for America in the 1890s: "On Sunday we encountered a very heavy gale of wind and rain. The rain was so strong that it blew the waves mountain high. Time after time the waves came sweeping the deck clear."

In a journal in the collection of the Walter Elwood Museum, Kindon wrote that he had a fiddle for entertainment on the crossing and "plenty of eatables," including ham, biscuits, jam, brandy and ginger ale.

Kindon found work at Burlington Carpet Mills in Mount Holly, New Jersey, but left there in 1892 to join the ranks of carpet workers in Amsterdam. Kindon faced "hard times" in the recession of 1893 but "started weaving" in 1894. He kept track of the lengths of carpet he wove each day and time spent servicing the loom. He translated the pay he received in dollars into English pounds.

He kept a record of the girls he courted. The 1910 city directory listed James Kindon, weaver, and his wife, Ada Gowey Kindon, living at 12 Eagle Street. At that time, immigrants from Poland, Italy, Lithuania, Russia and elsewhere were flocking to Amsterdam.

By the 1930s, the Kindons were living at 55 Stewart Street. James Kindon, still living on Stewart Street, retired from his duties as a weaver at Mohawk Carpet Mills in 1955, when he was eighty-one. He had worked sixty-two years at the plant, founded by brothers from England named Shuttleworth. Shortly before Kindon's retirement, Amsterdam's other

Designers working at an Amsterdam carpet mill. *Walter Elwood Museum.*

Opposite, top: Mohawk Carpet salesmen at a 1926 conference in Amsterdam. *Front row, left*: John V. Smeallie, who drove to his sales assignment in St. Louis in 1930, his automobile pulling a travel trailer. *Walter Elwood Museum.*

Opposite, bottom: Mohawk office women who served dinner at the 1926 salesmen's conference. *Walter Elwood Museum.*

A LOST WAY OF LIFE

A Group of Our Salesmen Who Attended the Mohawk Sales Conference
Front Row, L to R: J. Smeallie, O. Martin, J. Dohrman, H. Melsha,
J. Black, G. Hammond, F. Holliday, S. Ransopher, E. Earp, A. Grenier,
G. McDonald. Middle Row: J. Galligan, E. Peddie, J. Quigley, C. Skoug,
F. Geyer, M. Davidson, H. Lyon, W. Belknap, Jr., W. Malloy, J. McLean,
C. Edmonds. Top Row: R. Chapman, J. Galbraith, E. Kempf, F. Starkey,
G. Malone, T. Fogle, W. Keil, R. Arnold, R. Heffernan, H. Hammond, H. Townsend

Main Office Girls Who Served Dinner at McCleary Cafeteria for Mohawk Salesmen
From W. & J. Sloane Company, October 1926
1st Row- E. Janis, E. Bremer, E. Luneburg, M. Masten, M. Midler, E. Brown,
E. Belfance, F. Sager
2nd Row- D. Lane, D. Harrington, F. Tetlow, E. Murkey, H. Covey, E. Rotbell.
Back Row- E. Loder, M. Faulds, M. Stockwell, A. Stanton, E. Barnell.

major carpet factory, Bigelow Sanford, had announced it was leaving the city later that year. Kindon's son J. Artisan Kindon, who had become an assistant superintendent of Mohawk's tapestry division, died in May of that year. Father and son were active members of Masonic organizations. The Kindons worshipped at Second Presbyterian Church.

James Kindon died in April 1957 at age eighty-three. His wife, Ada, lived into the 1960s and was last reported living at a nursing home in Penn Yan, New York.

ON THE ROAD FOR MOHAWK

Carpet making was an industrial process. However, the finished product was a work of decorative art. A 1930 in-house publication called the *Mohawk Courier* contained praise from a New York City theater for a Mohawk Carpet Mills rug.

The 1930 *Courier* described how the firm's sales force was fanning out around the country. Sales director Z.L. Potter admitted that the nation had fallen on hard times, "but I pledge you personally and for all members of the sales organization that we will leave no stone unturned that will bring in business, start all Mohawk looms up again and give you the security of employment you desire."

There was a going-away dinner at Saltsman's Hotel in Ephratah for regional sales managers who were being dispatched to San Francisco, Philadelphia and St. Louis to promote the company's products.

Colonel G.H. Durston was assigned to San Francisco, and J. Ralph Blocher drew the Philadelphia assignment. "Invited but not present at the dinner because he was already enroute for his new home in St. Louis was John Smeallie," wrote the *Courier*. A picture showed Smeallie; his wife, Madge; and their daughters standing in front of an automobile attached to an impressive trailer. Smeallie reported the car and trailer made the 1,100-mile trip to St. Louis without "mar or trouble."

He added, "I snaked the trailer along at 45 and 50 miles per hour on straight concrete stretches and had absolutely no trouble in traffic, even in Cleveland, Indianapolis or St. Louis. We stopped for some meals and prepared others in transit, Mrs. Smeallie walking about the car and kitchen just as if she were at home. She claimed it rode much more comfortably than any sedan she was ever in and read a book enroute as well as drinking in the scenery."

A LOST WAY OF LIFE

John Van Derveer Smeallie was born in 1885, the son of insurance man James Smeallie and his wife, Ada. After high school, John worked three years at the *Amsterdam Morning Sentinel* newspaper and then joined his father in the insurance and real estate business. He was elected city treasurer as a Republican and served two terms, from 1912 through 1915.

Smeallie joined Mohawk Carpet Mills as purchasing agent and after some years went into advertising and sales promotion in 1926. In the 1930s, he started touring the country as head of Mohawk's lecture bureau, delivering speeches on the carpet industry to colleges and women's clubs and at promotional events. The *Recorder* wrote, "He was considered by many to be the foremost carpet authority in the industry."

By the 1940s, he and his family had moved to Forest Hills, an affluent section of Queens on Long Island. Mohawk had offices in New York City.

Smeallie collapsed and died from coronary thrombosis after finishing a carpet lecture to a group of people at a hotel in Grand Rapids, Michigan, on March 23, 1949. He was sixty-three. His sister Katherine had died in a similar fashion three years earlier as she was speaking to the Good Will Club in Amsterdam on April 3, 1946, telling of a recent trip to Mexico with her husband, physician Robert Simpson. She was fifty-seven.

MILL GIRLS

Modestly but eloquently, Sue Fraczek described her first day on the job at Bigelow Sanford's Amsterdam mill in the 1940s: "When I went to work, I was scared to death. It was my first time in a carpet mill. It was hot. It was noisy."

Fraczek was surprised to see herself as a young millworker in a still picture prominently featured in *Historic Views of the Carpet City*, the WMHT-TV documentary on Amsterdam first shown in 2000.

Co-producer Steve Dunn chose the picture of the young woman at the twisting machine to symbolize the documentary that he and I produced. Her photo appeared on the cover of WMHT's viewer magazine. It was used in newspaper articles and featured prominently on the covers of videocassettes and DVDs.

"It was a really good picture, technically good," Dunn recalled. "The black-and-white content expressed the whole theme—industrial workers in a milltown. I loved the way the spindles receded in the picture, and I loved the bandanna and the period clothes the woman wore."

Women winding yarn in an Amsterdam carpet mill. *Walter Elwood Museum.*

Fraczek did not recall having the photo taken and didn't know it existed until she saw it on television. The photo is one of two pictures of her in the collection of the Elwood Museum.

Dunn and I did not know the identity of the "mill girl" until several months after the documentary aired. Schoolteacher Gerry Brown stopped to talk with me at the Amsterdam Price Chopper supermarket and identified the person in the photo as her godmother and aunt.

Sue Fraczek's parents were Polish immigrants. Her dad worked at Mohawk Carpet in the city's East End, what was called Mohawk's Lower Mill. Mohawk also had a mill complex up the hill at Forest Avenue and Lyon Street in Rockton, the Upper Mill. Sue's mother, who died young, sometimes worked at Bigelow Sanford, the rug factory that bordered their Park Hill neighborhood.

Handling yarn and fabric became Fraczek's trade as a teenager. She took a power machine course at Vrooman Avenue School in 1940 and worked at

Wilton Card Stamping Machine
In Operation - 1923

A Jacquard loom card-stamping machine at Mohawk Carpet, 1923. *Walter Elwood Museum.*

Novak's shirt factory on Edson Street and the Amsterdam Coat Company in the city's West End.

Toward the end of World War II, she got her job running a twisting machine at Bigelow Sanford Building 54. The machine took three strands of woolen yarn and twisted the strands into stronger fibers that would be used in weaving carpets. The yarn left the twisting room on spools or bobbins.

Sue Fraczek of Amsterdam operating a yarn-twisting machine at Bigelow Sanford Carpet in the 1940s. *Walter Elwood Museum.*

A LOST WAY OF LIFE

Many factory workers, twisters or winders included, were paid on a piecework basis. Their pay was determined by the weight of the yarn-filled bobbins they produced. Fraczek recalled typically making forty-five dollars for forty hours' work, a lot less than the carpet weavers made. "They made good money," Fraczek said.

Fraczek stayed at Bigelow Sanford until the company left Amsterdam in 1955. She was hired for a similar job at Mohawk/Mohasco Carpet, which lasted another six years.

She then found employment using a sewing machine at White Stag in the East End, where underwear was made, and Mohawk Sportswear in the West End. She retired from millwork in 1989. Fraczek is not the only Amsterdam mill veteran who can say, "Almost every job I lost was because the company closed or moved out."

Outside the mills, Fraczek led a full life. She never married but spent countless hours helping to raise children in her extended family. She was known for having a great eye for selecting excellent gifts for nieces and nephews. After leaving the mills, she enjoyed peace and quiet and was a voracious reader, especially enjoying the classics.

Ann Peconie, executive director of the Elwood Museum, said you could learn a lot from the dress, jewelry and demeanor of women photographed in the mills.

Peconie said one of her favorite pictures shows a woman tending a machine, looking at the camera and sporting a bracelet and high heels. "I make jokes saying the woman seems to be saying she would rather be in another place at another time."

Women could have only certain jobs. Peconie said she never heard of a female carpet weaver. Women often were creelers. Creelers made sure the loom was tied into yarn spindles or bobbins.

"My grandmother had a little knife around her finger to cut and then tie the yarn," Peconie said. Her grandmother added that weavers sometimes were mean men.

"Women worked when they were sick, when they were pregnant," Peconie said. "They tried to hide their conditions from the bosses. They only had stools to sit on, no backs. If a woman was ill, other women would cover, letting the woman [who was sick] lie down on the factory floor on top of her coat. Camaraderie developed over time."

Amsterdam native Alberta Zierak Fondacaro said:

When I was a child, my aunts would bring me yarn dolls that were made from scraps of wool. They lied about their ages and started working in the factories when they were youngsters to help support the family. I still have a discarded bolt of yarn. They even showed me how to determine a fine woolen rug from a poorly weaved one.

Back in the '50s, you could first look at the back of the rug. The weave of a less expensive rug would be wider and flat whereas the weave of a better rug was tighter and had a different look. If you bent the carpet in the front you could actually see the difference in loops. I certainly wasn't any expert but just a child who took an interest in my aunts' lives. These women were pioneers who didn't complain of hardships.

CARPETS AND COMPUTERS

Mark Thomann, who has spent much of his working life on restorations of classic carpets, is skeptical of the frequently mentioned idea that paper cards used to control carpet weaving directly foreshadowed development of the computer. Thomann is owner of Stuart Jackson LLC, a firm that re-creates historic floor coverings.

Thomann said that some carpet looms use paper punch cards, as did early computers. In the weaving process, these cards determine the position of each strand of yarn. But Thomann said, "I have never seen evidence that someone familiar with that industrial technology was at all involved in making computers."

Thousands of cardboard cards were used to weave carpets in Amsterdam years ago on what were called Jacquard looms, named for Joseph Marie Jacquard of Lyon, France, who came up with improvements to the mechanical loom in 1801.

Jacquard looms had a chain of punched cards that were tied together to determine whether yarn of a particular color would be visible or buried beneath other yarn.

The website of the Computer History Museum states that English mathematician Charles Babbage did use punch cards similar to those utilized on Jacquard looms when developing his "Analytical Engine" to perform computations. Babbage died in 1871.

The holes in the paper cards on Jacquard looms originally were punched manually. The Elwood museum has a 1923 picture of a female factory worker manually punching the holes. In the heyday of Amsterdam carpet production, the cards were punched by machine.

A LOST WAY OF LIFE

Men sorting wool at an Amsterdam carpet mill. *Walter Elwood Museum.*

Thomann said there are still Jacquard looms in operation, and the holes that determine where the yarn goes are punched with computer control today.

Jacquard looms made it easier to weave carpets using a variety of colors. In an advertising display used by Mohawk Carpet years ago, its North Shore Wilton brand promised the availability of fourteen colorful patterns. Axminster carpet also was known for use of many colors and patterns. In its Amsterdam days, Mohawk used the slogan "On the well covered floor, every square inch counts."

Amsterdam's major carpet manufacturers, Bigelow Sanford and Mohawk/Mohasco, left the former Carpet City decades ago. Bigelow Sanford moved out in 1955. Mohasco, a name created when Mohawk merged with carpet maker Alexander Smith, staged a more orderly retreat, closing its last Amsterdam offices in the 1980s.

Why the mills left has been a hot topic. Some people blame the mill owners; some blame the unions. Unlike the unionized North, unions were not prevalent in the South. The pay rates were lower in the South and

A weaver at a Wilton Jacquard loom at Mohawk Carpet. The cards laced together on top of the machine controlled the pattern of the carpet. *Walter Elwood Museum.*

offshore, where many mills ultimately relocated. Southern communities also offered tax concessions.

Thomann contended one of the reasons the carpet industry left the North was a shift in production technique from weaving to tufting. In the weaving process, yarns are simultaneously interlaced, eliminating the need for a backing. The Carpet and Rug Institute describes tufting as "the process of creating textiles, especially carpet, on specialized multi-needle sewing machines. Several hundred needles stitch hundreds of rows of pile yarn tufts through a backing fabric called the primary backing."

Tufting produces carpet more quickly than weaving. Thomann said the tufting machines were too huge and heavy to fit into the old multistoried mill buildings in Amsterdam and other northern cities. According to the Carpet and Rug Institute, tufted carpet accounts for 95 percent of carpets made today.

A weaver at an Axminster loom at Mohawk Carpet. *Walter Elwood Museum.*

Some carpets are still woven at Eden, North Carolina; Landrum, South Carolina; and Bloomsburg, Pennsylvania. England has seen a bit of resurgence in woven carpet production. And today, Thomann said, there are female carpet weavers.

Bloomsburg Carpet advertises that it maintains the tradition of weaving carpet in the styles that were made years ago, including Axminster and

Wilton. These names derive from locations in England, where the rugs were first produced. There is an Axminster in Devonshire and a Wilton in Wiltshire.

A MOHAWK KID

My grandfather, Harry Cudmore, came to Amsterdam from Torrington, Devonshire, England, in 1911 accompanied by his eldest son, Stanley. Harry wove silk for Fownes Brothers, an Amsterdam glove mill.

My grandmother Elizabeth and the rest of the family (Gladys, Winifred, Percy and my father, Clarence) crossed the ocean in 1912. One more child, Vera, was born over here.

The family story was that Elizabeth had been expected to sail (albeit in steerage) on the ill-fated *Titanic* but was not eager to leave England. The family missed the *Titanic*. After the *Titanic* sank, White Star Line pressed the old *Majestic* (launched in 1889) back into service. The Cudmores came over on the *Majestic*.

The family passed through Ellis Island and settled on Eagle Street in the East End of Amsterdam, in a double house also occupied by house painter Robert Brown (I was named for him) and his wife, Beatrice, who was Harry Cudmore's sister.

The bumptious ragman Harry Demsky lived a few doors away with his wife, Bryna, and a family that included young Isadore Demsky or Danielovitch, who would become the actor Kirk Douglas.

My dad, Clarence Cudmore, attended Fourth Ward School, built in 1894 on Vrooman Avenue, between Main Street and the Mohawk River. It was an imposing four-story structure.

School principal James Adams let Dad and other boys fix up the school's top floor for basketball. Dad said it was the one time he enjoyed being called to the principal's office when Adams explained his concept for a gym.

Dad used to joke that he did such a good job in fourth grade that they let him take fourth grade a second year. Fourth Ward School itself was destroyed in a spectacular fire in about 1940. My sister Arlene was a student there at the time.

As a young man, Dad sang in minstrel shows and other theatrical productions at East Main Street Methodist Episcopal Church and hummed and sang until he died.

A LOST WAY OF LIFE

Right: The author and his father, Clarence Cudmore, a Wilton weaver for Mohawk Carpet. *Author's collection.*

Below: Mohawk Mills Association children's party at the State Armory, Amsterdam. *Walter Elwood Museum.*

WE ARE THE MOHAWK KIDDIES

WE ARE THE MOHAWK KIDDIES

Mohawk Mills Association Kiddies Party
State Armory, Amsterdam

His first factory job was at General Electric in Schenectady, and it looked like the start of a promising career. However, he was laid off in the Depression. He had a government job at Amsterdam's city hall for a time.

He said it was his English roots that helped him then find employment in the Depression at Mohawk Carpet Mills, owned by people of English origin.

He started as a creeler and became a foreman of the creelers and sparehands. He was given the option of going forward in management or qualifying for one of the top production jobs. He chose the latter and became a Wilton carpet weaver.

SHIFT WORK

Dad alternated shifts on a weekly basis, working 6:00 a.m. to 2:00 p.m. the first week and 2:00 p.m. to 10:00 p.m. the next week. Sometimes he worked the shift he hated, 10:00 p.m. to 6:00 a.m.

The Lower Mill of Mohawk Carpet along the Mohawk River. *Walter Elwood Museum.*

A LOST WAY OF LIFE

The Upper Mill of Mohawk Carpet at Forest Avenue and Lyon Street in Amsterdam's Rockton section. *Walter Elwood Museum.*

For many years, my father's partner, the man who had the opposite shift on the loom they shared, was Sam Bonafede, who played in a band. That worked to Dad's advantage. He worked mostly days and Bonafede worked mostly nights, as long as he could have crucial nights off to play in the band.

At first, we were renters in a four-family house owned by Albert and Lillian Wojcik on Pulaski Street, a short but steep walk or drive from the factory down by the river where Dad worked. In the winter, the Lower Mill employees chatted nervously about whether people were "making it" up steep Vrooman Avenue hill at quitting time. There were alternate routes. A carpet weaver, as Sue Fraczek said, made good money for a mill hand. In 1957, we moved farther up the hill to our own home in a suburban-like setting on Peter Lane.

Like many millworkers, Dad prided himself on being quick. When he was working days, he could leave the mill, head to Nicholas Fratangelo's nearby East Main Street barbershop and get a haircut. Like me, he was pretty bald at an early age so a haircut didn't take too long. He would be home before 2:45 p.m.

Thursday, he headed to the Forbes Street Market. Mother by then had called in "the order," and Dad picked it up and was home by 2:30 p.m.

When Dad worked nights, he hurried home on Fridays and by 10:15 p.m. was sitting at a TV tray eating pizza that his wife, Julia, had made, watching the Friday night fights on television. Mother, a New York State native, was not Italian, but she was an excellent cook and made her own pizza.

There was one time when I was in grade school that our class was taken on a tour of Bigelow Sanford's carpet mill. What I remember best was crossing over a city street on one of its enclosed walkways. I never went inside Mohawk Mills where my father worked at a Wilton loom.

When I learned to drive, I was sometimes granted the car on Friday nights, but the categorical imperative was I had to be parked on Elk Street at Mohawk Mills a few minutes before 10:00 p.m. to wait for Dad to emerge.

Dad complained about the introduction of "speed looms," apparently an effort to stave off the transition to tufted carpet. Carpet production at Mohasco in Amsterdam ceased in 1968, but Dad, a loyal union member, was able to continue working at other tasks around the mill until 1973.

He had a few months before Social Security kicked in. One of his old East End friends, Pete Riccio, who helped Kirk Douglas go to college, was the head of the unemployment office then and made sure Dad kept getting his benefits. My father earned his high school equivalency diploma while looking for work but never got another job. He enjoyed his twenty-year retirement and his family until a year or two before he passed. He died in a nursing home in 1994.

He was suffering from a form of dementia that reminded me of the *Star Trek* episode in which a former star ship captain is allowed to continue living in a dream world. Just before he died, Dad thought his male nurse's aide was a composite of all his friends and even enemies from years ago.

Jose said Dad would sometimes call him "that bloody fool" and worse, but other times Dad talked about catching the trolley car to go downtown and delighted Jose and the nursing home floor with his vocalizing.

PAVED WITH GOLD

Anthony "Tony" Murdico was born in Reggio Calabria, Italy, in 1915. Murdico and his family came to Amsterdam in 1923, and Tony got a job at Mohawk Carpet in 1929, when he was only fourteen. Like Alberta

An Amsterdam carpet mill dye house. Union leader Anthony Murdico said no one wanted to work there. *Walter Elwood Museum.*

Two doctors and three nurses staffed the Mohawk Carpet dispensary in 1923. *Left to right*: Dr. L.H. Finch, Mrs. F. Sparks, Miss M. MacKenzie, Mrs. L. Finchout and Dr. Canna. *Walter Elwood Museum.*

Carpets in boxes ready for shipment. *Walter Elwood Museum.*

Fondacaro's aunts, he lied about his age. He progressed through the ranks to become a Wilton weaver.

"I come from a very poor family, and we had to go to work," Murdico said. "For me coming from another country and going to work in the mill, I thought the streets over here were paved with gold."

The mill unionized in the 1940s, and Murdico was named shop steward. He became recording secretary of the Textile Workers Union of America local in 1946. In 1952, he was elected president of the union local and held that post until 1981.

"When I became president of the union it was the best thing that could happen to me," Murdico said. "A foreigner coming over from Italy."

What was called the "big strike" took place in 1952, when carpet workers were on the picket lines for twelve weeks at factories in northern states.

"We got eleven cents [an hour raise]," Murdico said.

Work in a carpet mill could be a dirty job. One problem spot was the dye house where woolen yarn was dumped in huge vats. Murdico said, "Everybody hated to work in the dye house. Everybody."

A LOST WAY OF LIFE

The carpet mill could be a dangerous place. Anthrax was a specific concern, Murdico said. "Every time you got a scratch in the mill, or a cut, or any kind of wound at all you had to report it immediately. Because anthrax travels around the mill where there's wool."

DRINKING, GAMBLING AND OTHER ENTERTAINMENT

In its carpet-making heyday, Amsterdam was a center for drinking and gambling. After hours in the factory, millworkers looked forward to a shot and a beer at the end of the day. When the factory whistle sounded, streams of workers headed home, but some of them headed for their favorite taverns. The attitude of the general population toward heavy drinking then may have been more tolerant, but drinking took its toll on many families.

Illegal gambling was huge. When people saw you in the morning, their first question was to ask if you knew the day's winning number by saying, "What came out?" Candy stores and newsrooms fronted for card games and bookmaking. Numbers takers operated inside the mills.

The carpet mills themselves sponsored more wholesome entertainment—choruses, bands, theatrical shows, sporting events, children's parties and dinners for millworkers, sometimes held inside the factory.

The millworkers gave one another nicknames, many of which are unprintable or at least politically incorrect. Our family's nickname was Cuddy, although my uncle Percy Cudmore spelled the word "Cudy" on his bowling shirts.

In an interview recorded in 1999 for the WMHT documentary on Amsterdam, Tony Murdico and I touched on the issue of nicknames as we looked at pictures taken when the mills were still in high gear. Murdico died in 2008:

> *CUDMORE: I think I see a guy selling numbers down in the street there, Tony.*
> *MURDICO: Yeah. Here's where your dad worked. Your dad worked in this mill. He was buying a number that day. (laughter)*
> *CUDMORE: He could have been.*
> *MURDICO: Cross that off. (more laughter)*
> *CUDMORE: It sounds like in some ways these were the happiest years of your life.*
> *MURDICO: It was. It was.*

WE DO NOT BOAST OF OUR EVENTS
WE BOAST OF OUR PRODUCTION

The Henry Bianchi Family at Mohawks' Annual Field Day at Jollyland Park

A LOST WAY OF LIFE

Workers having a banquet inside a carpet mill. *Walter Elwood Museum.*

Opposite, top: Five women performing at a Mohawk Carpet employee theatrical production, circa 1920s. *Walter Elwood Museum.*

Opposite, bottom: The Henry Bianchi family attending a Mohawk Carpet field day. *Walter Elwood Museum.*

> *CUDMORE: I mean the gang at the mill. You calling each other names—Fatso and Skinny and names we can't repeat. The taking of the numbers. The women—there were a lot of pretty women who worked in these mills.*
> *MURDICO: Oh there were pretty, pretty women. The creelers were awful pretty. Ask more questions about it. I can answer almost anything. Twenty-seven years I was president of the union. And I had fifty-one years in the mill! Fifty-one years. I got a gold watch, fifty-one years, I got a gold watch.*

Anthropologist Susan R. Dauria of Bloomsburg University of Pennsylvania studied the final years of the carpet mill culture in Amsterdam for her doctoral dissertation at the University at Albany.

Bigelow Sanford's Amsterdam headquarters, the Clock Building, at Christmas. The building is still there. *Walter Elwood Museum.*

Opposite, top: Trucks were constantly on Amsterdam streets shuttling between Mohawk's two factory sites, the Upper Mill and the Lower Mill. *Walter Elwood Museum.*

Opposite, bottom: A popular Amsterdam tavern in the early 1900s was Flanagan's Café at Church and Reid Streets. *Montgomery County Department of History and Archives.*

Dauria said, "If you would go by any of the mills during the day you could hear the looms. You could hear them smacking. It was like a heartbeat. You could feel the town. It was alive. It was working. It was producing. And

A LOST WAY OF LIFE

people talk about that all the time, that feeling. The whole town was just sort of throbbing. It was exciting."

Amsterdam carpets made it at least twice to the White House. The Liberty Rug was one of twenty Axminster carpets woven in Amsterdam by the Shuttleworth mills, the predecessor of Mohawk Carpet, to mark the initial floodlighting ceremony at the Statue of Liberty in New York in 1916. The rug was then presented to President Woodrow Wilson for his bedroom at the White House. In 1947, a Chenille rug from Mohawk Carpet showing the presidential seal was produced for President Harry Truman's Oval Office.

Part II

LOST LINKS TO FAMOUS PEOPLE

JOHN PHILIP SOUSA AND HIS SPECIAL FRIEND IN ST. JOHNSVILLE

John Philip Sousa, the "March King" who composed "The Stars and Stripes Forever," unsuccessfully courted a woman from the Mohawk Valley and remained her special friend through the years.

Jessie Zoller was born in 1856 in the town of Minden on the south side of the Mohawk River. Jessie was the daughter of prosperous egg farmer Abram Zoller and his wife, Alma Tuttle Zoller.

The Zoller family had migrated to Minden from Switzerland before the American Revolution, and family members were prominent citizens. After the Civil War, Abram Zoller secured a high post in the U.S. Treasury, and his wife and daughter lived with him in Washington.

Jessie met Sousa when they both were students at a music and art conservatory in the capital city. Sousa was born in Washington in 1854. His father was Portuguese and Spanish, and his mother was Bavarian.

The late St. Johnsville historian Anita Smith said Jessie's father did not encourage Sousa: "The story is told that Mr. Zoller called John a young upstart musician who would never amount to much and certainly wasn't good enough for his Jessie."

Jessie earned a degree at Vassar College in Poughkeepsie and then enrolled in the Leipzig Conservatory in Germany. Smith was told by local sources that Jessie was sent to Europe by her father to keep her away from Sousa. She and her mother spent fourteen years in Europe. She was presented to the emperor of Germany. Her father joined them for the last four years abroad. Jessie became fluent in German, Italian and French. She also was trained as an opera singer.

Smith wrote, "When Jessie returned to America she had 14 trunks filled with beautiful clothing, jewels, opera costumes, laces and many other lovely items."

The Zollers went to Omaha and then Chicago, where Jessie continued her studies. In Chicago, she saw Sousa once again.

Sousa had married Jane van Middlesworth Bellis in 1879. Bellis was a singer from Philadelphia, and Sousa met her when he was playing violin in a theater where she performed. They had three children.

In 1880, Sousa was named to head the U.S. Marine Band at the White House, and his reputation as a bandleader and composer soared. He formed his own band in 1892. The *New York Times* wrote, "The wide travels of the band throughout the United States…have contributed toward the furtherance of musical education in the nation."

A letter from Sousa to Jessie in 1899 said he was still interested in her: "It has been 12 years since I saw you last, but it seems like a thousand years to me." He added that he "must see" her again. "Anytime I can be of service to you, please command me."

Sousa asked Jessie what she had been doing all the years they were apart. According to Smith, Jessie replied that she had a placid lifestyle. Sousa responded that his lifestyle "is filled with electricity and that he has to be a human dynamo."

Jessie's mother died in 1902. Jessie and her father moved back to the Mohawk Valley and settled on Kingsbury Avenue and then on Ann Street in St. Johnsville. Her father was occasionally in the local news as executor of the will of a friend named Solomon Miller. Miller had left the bulk of a $50,000 estate to Amanda Pike, a woman the deceased regarded as his adopted daughter. Other members of the family contested the will, and the issue was apparently still not settled when Abram Zoller died in 1906. His obituary noted that Jessie "watched with devoted care" over her father's "declining years."

When Sousa was near St. Johnsville, located on a railroad main line, he visited Jessie, sometimes, it was said, getting the train to make an unscheduled stop. Village residents said the "March King" looked very dapper in his dress clothes replete with medals and white gloves.

Jessie was cultured and talented, the foremost authority in her village on language, music and art. She never married but was active as a music and art teacher until 1928 and then lived a more reclusive life.

LOST LINKS TO FAMOUS PEOPLE

John Philip Sousa, America's top march composer and bandleader, had a long friendship with a woman in the Mohawk Valley. *Library of Congress.*

Sousa lived his later years in Sands Point on Long Island. According to one of his biographers, Paul E. Bierley, the bandleader once said, "When you hear of Sousa retiring, you will hear of Sousa dead."

Sousa did not retire. He died in 1932 at age seventy-seven in a hotel in Reading, Pennsylvania, after conducting a band rehearsal the previous day. He was buried at Congressional Cemetery in Washington.

Left: John Philip Sousa frequently visited this highly educated St. Johnsville woman. Jessie Zoller was an art and music teacher. *Margaret Reaney Library.*

Below: Jessie Zoller's painting of a hay wagon is among her art works displayed at St. Johnsville's Community House. *Kathy Snyder.*

LOST LINKS TO FAMOUS PEOPLE

Jessie's 1938 newspaper obituary said she had been one of Sousa's closest friends. The *St. Johnsville Enterprise* wrote on its front page, "She was a quiet, unassuming lady, whose friendship was enjoyed by many."

A member of the Christian Science Church, Jessie died at the home of her cousin, Irving Devendorf, and was buried at Fort Plain Cemetery.

Smith said a few people in St. Johnsville have paintings and pieces of china that Jessie created. Industrialist Joseph Reaney bought the largest collection of her paintings, and they are displayed at the St. Johnsville Community House, which houses village government offices and a large room for community events.

At a St. Johnsville fashion show in the 1950s that paid tribute to the coronation of Queen Elizabeth II in Great Britain, a relative of Jessie's named Joan Devendorf wore the gown Jessie wore when she was presented to the emperor of Germany in the late 1800s.

Artist Jessie Zoller's version of a detail called *The Two Cherubs* from a 1512 painting by Raphael. Zoller said the cherubs represented her and her friend, John Philip Sousa. The picture is displayed at the St. Johnsville Community House. *Kathy Snyder.*

Jessie's version of *The Two Cherubs*, a detail from a famous Raphael painting, is one of the pictures on display at the Community House. Local lore has it that Jessie said the cherubs represent her and her friend Sousa.

ANITA SMITH

St. Johnsville village and town historian Anita Bellen Smith, source for much of the information for this story, died in May 2015. She was ninety. Smith had previously served as Montgomery County historian. She wrote history books and articles and prepared many National Register of Historic Places forms for buildings in Montgomery County. She and her late husband, Frederick Smith, operated a market and then a liquor store in St. Johnsville.

Smith was county historian in 1980, when actress and controversial activist Jane Fonda made a surprise visit to Fonda while tracing her family history. Current county historian Kelly Farquhar said Smith took Fonda and some others from her family on a tour of the Caughnawaga Cemetery in the village.

In a letter to the editor in 2013, Smith wrote, "History isn't dull, because it's being made fresh every day."

ED SULLIVAN'S AMSTERDAM ROOTS

Television star and newspaper columnist Ed Sullivan's parents were married in Amsterdam on September 22, 1896, five years before he was born.

Ed's mother was Elizabeth F. Smith, whose family resided at 33 Garden Street. His father, Peter A. Sullivan, was living in New York City working as a customs inspector when he married Elizabeth. The wedding took place at St. Mary's Roman Catholic Church with the Reverend John McIncrow celebrating Mass.

Elizabeth was an amateur painter and "a young lady of many graces." Elizabeth and Peter were described in newspaper wedding coverage as popular young people. Elizabeth was twenty-one, and Peter was thirty-six.

There was a "bountiful repast" at the home of the bride's parents, Mr. and Mrs. Edward Smith. Minch's orchestra entertained. The newly married couple left on the 5:23 p.m. train for their new home in New York City.

THE SULLIVANS

Peter's father was Florence Sullivan, who came to Saratoga Springs from Glengarriff, Ireland, near Cork, in 1851. According to a genealogical report, Florence made the crossing on the *Fidelia*, a famine or coffin

Pioneer television star Ed Sullivan (right) with comedian Bob Newhart in 1961. Sullivan's parents came from Amsterdam. *Kobal Collection at Art Resource in New York.*

ship, so called because many immigrants died on these vessels during the long voyage.

Florence was a shoemaker and a coachman and later worked on the Erie Canal. He married an Irish immigrant named Margaret McNulty in 1853.

The Sullivan family headstone at St. Mary's Cemetery in Fort Johnson, New York. Ed Sullivan's twin brother, Daniel, is among those buried there. *Kathy Snyder.*

In the 1870 census, the family was living in Saratoga Springs, and Peter was ten years old.

When Florence died at age fifty-seven in 1883, his widow, Margaret, moved to Cornell Street in Amsterdam with her children. Later a neighborhood of Polish immigrants, at that time that section was an Irish American enclave nicknamed Cork Hill.

Peter was listed as a broom maker in the 1890 and 1891 city directories. Although he did not finish high school, he was third ward supervisor serving on the county board in 1892 and 1893.

In the news story on his marriage, Peter is described as "an Amsterdam boy." His younger brother Florence, named after their father, was assistant district attorney in 1896. In 1899, Florence delivered a talk at St. Mary's Institute on Irish patriotism. In 1901, he became Amsterdam city attorney. In 1904, he moved to New York City and worked as a successful trial lawyer there until his death in 1941. He was among those buried in the Sullivan family plot at St. Mary's Cemetery in Fort Johnson, west of Amsterdam.

Two other brothers of Peter Sullivan had notable careers. Daniel was a U.S. Army colonel in both world wars and served as a New York State assistant attorney general. Charles became a civil engineer.

INFANT DEATHS

Peter and Elizabeth Sullivan gave their first son the traditional family name of Florence in 1899. He died in infancy in New York, and his body was sent to Amsterdam for burial at St. Mary's Cemetery that September.

Edward Vincent Sullivan and his twin brother, Daniel, were born on East 114th Street in an Irish and Jewish neighborhood of Harlem on September 28, 1901. Daniel died in July 1902, and his body also was taken by train to Amsterdam for burial. When Ed was five, his family moved from Harlem to Port Chester, New York.

DID ED SULLIVAN EVER LIVE IN AMSTERDAM?

Amsterdam attorney and historian Robert Going said, "According to my grandmother, whose voice should not be considered authoritative, Ed's family lived here off and on until he was about seven, and she pointed out the apartment they lived in." The second-floor apartment she pointed to was 149 East Main Street, across from St. Mary's Church, over what old-timers today remember as Johnnie's Seafood.

Kathy Smith of Amsterdam said her father, James V. Smith, was Ed Sullivan's first cousin. Kathy was told that Ed Sullivan did spend some time living in Amsterdam when he was young but was not told where he lived.

Ed was a high school athlete and student sports reporter for St. Mary's High School in Port Chester but turned down a chance to go to college, according to an online biography. An uncle, perhaps Florence Sullivan, had offered to pay the bill.

Ed went on to become a newspaper columnist and then a radio and television star. He began dating Sylvia Weinstein, although both families were said to be opposed to a Catholic-Jewish wedding. They married in a civil ceremony in 1930, and their daughter Elizabeth, or Betty, was born that year. She was named after Ed's mother.

Sullivan's long-running television variety program, at first called *The Toast of the Town*, debuted in 1948. It became *The Ed Sullivan Show* in 1955 and was a CBS Sunday night staple. His show often introduced mainstream American audiences to groundbreaking performers, most famously four appearances by the Beatles in the 1960s. In 1968, the theater where he broadcast the show was renamed the Ed Sullivan Theater.

Kathy Smith said when she was getting ready for life after high school in the 1960s, she wrote a letter to Ed Sullivan asking if he thought she should move to New York City. He advised against it, and Smith remained in Amsterdam.

CBS canceled Ed Sullivan's show in 1971. His wife, Sylvia, died in 1973, and Ed died in 1974. He is buried at Ferncliff Cemetery about twenty-five miles north of midtown Manhattan in Hartsdale, New York.

SAM GOLDWYN
AND GLOVERSVILLE

Samuel Goldwyn, one of the movie moguls who led Metro Goldwyn Mayer (MGM) in the last century, lived in Gloversville as a young man.

Born Schmuel Gelbfish in Warsaw, Poland's Jewish ghetto around 1879, he made his way to the United States in 1898. Samuel Goldfish, as he was known by then, had learned the glove trade in Europe and heard that Gloversville was a center of that business and home to many Jewish glove-cutters.

According to historian Peter Betz, Goldfish's first Gloversville job was as a sweeper at the Louis Meyers and Son glove factory at West Pine and South Main Streets. He earned three dollars a week. He made more money when he became a glove cutter at Joseph Moses Bacmo Gloves. He went to Gloversville Business College to improve his manners and speaking skills.

He became a foreman for the Elite Glove Company and eventually a salesman for Elite. Before he was thirty, he was earning $15,000 a year. He sent money to his family in Europe, and his two younger brothers came to America and also sold gloves.

Goldfish was promoted to sales manager for Elite and transferred his offices to New York City, where he was exposed to the first productions of the movie industry. He started Goldwyn Pictures in 1917 and changed his name to Samuel Goldwyn.

LOST LINKS TO FAMOUS PEOPLE

Movie mogul Sam Goldwyn of MGM in 1938. He worked at glove mills in Gloversville as a young man. *Kobal Collection at Art Resource NY.*

Goldwyn did not produce films for MGM but did produce movies for his own company, Samuel Goldwyn Productions. Among them were *Hans Christian Anderson*, *Guys and Dolls*, *Porgy and Bess* and *The Best Years of Our Lives*. Goldwyn died in 1974.

BACK TO GLOVERSVILLE

On October 30, 1945, Goldwyn came back to Gloversville and attended a dinner at the Kingsborough Hotel. He told the *Leader Herald*, "I have a great affection for this town. This is the place that gave me my first start in life." He had not been there, he said, since 1906.

Postcard view of Gloversville's Kingsborough Hotel, where Sam Goldwyn was the guest of honor at a 1945 dinner. The structure has been converted into an apartment building. *Author's collection.*

LOST LINKS TO FAMOUS PEOPLE

Goldwyn originally came to Gloversville as a teenager: "I not only got my first job here but stayed long enough to get my citizenship papers, which is perhaps the greatest gift to any man to become a citizen of this great country."

Goldwyn was invited to Gloversville in 1945 by Vern Steele, program chairman for the men's club of the Kingsborough Presbyterian Church. Steele had sent the invitation when Goldwyn was visiting Saratoga Springs.

Goldwyn was eager to return. He and writer Alexander Woollcott had planned a trip to Gloversville some years prior, but Woollcott died in 1943 before the trip could take place. Woollcott apparently had spent some time in Gloversville when Goldwyn lived there.

At the hotel, Goldwyn met with Albert Aaron, who had provided Goldwyn his first job in Gloversville. Also on hand was Jacob Liebglid, who taught a penniless Goldwyn the glove trade in Hamburg, Germany, after Goldwyn had run away from his Warsaw home. Liebglid also raised enough money from the Jewish community in Hamburg to get Goldwyn a ticket to England, the first stop on Goldwyn's passage to America. In 1945, Liebglid lived at the Kingsborough Hotel.

Goldwyn said, "When I was a boy, my one outstanding ambition was to get enough money to have dinner in the Hotel Kingsborough. And after that I wanted to stroll through the lobby, back and forth in front of the window and watch the pretty girls as they walked up and down the street. I realized my ambition but couldn't resist the impulse to do it again tonight when I was in the lobby."

The hotel closed many years ago, and the building on South Main Street today is the Kingsboro Apartments.

TEDDY ROOSEVELT IN THE MOHAWK VALLEY

O ver two thousand people turned out to see Theodore Roosevelt in 1896, according to historian Peter Betz, when the then New York City police commissioner came to support Republican congressional candidate Lucius Littauer in Gloversville.

Even bigger crowds showed up when Roosevelt barnstormed the Mohawk Valley during his own campaign for governor in 1898.

When Roosevelt arrived in Johnstown on October 22, 1898, mill whistles blew for a half hour. When he got to Gloversville later that day, he was greeted by an enthusiastic throng of seven thousand.

The *Amsterdam Recorder* began its coverage of Roosevelt's October 29, 1898 tour of Mohawk River cities in St. Johnsville. There his four-car campaign train was met by former congressman John Sanford and the newspaper's publisher, William Kline.

When the train stopped in Fort Plain, the Old Fort Plain Band performed and cadets from the local military school, Clinton Liberal Institute, paraded. The engineer wanted to meet the candidate so on the trip from Fort Plain to Fonda, Roosevelt rode in the cab of the locomotive. Some 1,500 people greeted the train in Fonda.

In Amsterdam, the crowd at the train station was estimated at two thousand with another five thousand lining the route of a parade from Railroad Street to the Opera House on East Main near Walnut Street. The Thirteenth Brigade Band led the march.

LOST LINKS TO FAMOUS PEOPLE

Governor Theodore Roosevelt addressing a crowd at the 1899 Fulton County Fair in Johnstown. *Fulton County Museum.*

The throng assembled to hear Roosevelt was too big for the Opera House, and some men may have been miffed that the first six rows were reserved for "the ladies." Not having the vote, women often were discouraged from attending political rallies. But since the candidate was a war hero and a Republican, wrote the *Recorder*, the ladies were allowed.

From June through August 1898, Colonel Roosevelt had been an officer in a volunteer cavalry unit in the Spanish-American War called the Rough Riders. Mason Mitchell, an actor who had served with the Rough Riders, gave the local crowd a graphic description of fighting at Santiago, Cuba.

Amsterdam's National Guard unit, Company H, had left the newly built South Side Armory in May for the war. The guardsmen got as far as the state of Florida, but the war ended before the local soldiers could be deployed to the combat zone.

In his Amsterdam speech, Colonel Roosevelt strongly critiqued the Democratic Party's New York City machine, Tammany Hall. A week later,

Roosevelt was elected governor, carrying Amsterdam by 422 votes. It was not a Republican sweep; Amsterdam elected a Democrat, Zerah H. Westbrook, as mayor that year, .

The September 6, 1899 *Albany Evening Journal* reported the largest crowd ever seen at the Fulton County Fair when Governor Roosevelt stopped by. The event was photographed, and the picture is in the collection of the Fulton County Museum.

Roosevelt visited Amsterdam in October 1900 as he campaigned to be vice president and was enthusiastically greeted, delivering another stirring address at the Opera House.

Elected as President William McKinley's vice president in 1900, Roosevelt became president in 1901 when McKinley was assassinated. Roosevelt learned McKinley had died while on a trek in the Adirondacks.

LITTAUER CONNECTION

Young Teddy Roosevelt had roomed with Lucius Littauer of the Gloversville glove-making family when both were students at Harvard. Elected to Congress in 1896, Littauer was a staunch Republican and an advocate for high tariffs on foreign-made gloves, according to Barbara McMartin in her book, *The Glove Cities*.

The *Gloversville Leader* reported in 1900 that Roosevelt told the Harvard Club that Littauer was his most intimate personal friend and closest political advisor.

There was speculation that Littauer would be named to Roosevelt's cabinet. But Littauer was accused of using his position as a congressman to get a contract for his company for gloves for the army, according to McMartin. The charge was never proved, although McMartin said the scandal prevented Littauer from getting a cabinet post in Roosevelt's administration. Littauer chose not to seek reelection to Congress in 1906.

AFTER THE PRESIDENCY

Roosevelt served as president through 1909. He visited the Mohawk Valley again in 1910 to campaign for Republican candidates for state office, speaking again at Amsterdam's Opera House on October 27. He proceeded by train to a tumultuous reception in Little Falls. The *Utica Herald Dispatch* reported there was a "great outburst of cheering by the crowd and a rush to get near Colonel Roosevelt." Millworkers were given time off to see the former president. After a motorcade and rally at a local theater, the colonel was presented with a box of quartz crystals, sometimes called Little Falls or Herkimer diamonds.

Roosevelt and his handpicked successor, William Howard Taft, gradually had a falling out. Not able to secure the Republican nomination, Roosevelt made an unsuccessful presidential bid on a third-party ticket in 1912, resulting in a victory for Democratic presidential candidate Woodrow Wilson.

LAST TRIP

Roosevelt's last reported trip to the Mohawk Valley was in 1914. That year, he was barnstorming with Progressive Party gubernatorial candidate and college professor Frederick Davenport. Roosevelt's tour began in St. Johnsville and proceeded by automobile to Amsterdam.

The colonel told an enthusiastic crowd at the Opera House, "We have got to have laws to prevent children from working. We have to have laws to protect the conditions under which a man should work. We have to have laws that guard against an excess of hours of labor for women kind." He argued that the state would not have effective government "under the combination of the two old party machines."

Roosevelt and his entourage had dinner at the home of E. Watson Gardiner, an Amsterdam wool dealer. The former president also stopped in Fultonville, Canajoharie, Fort Plain, Johnstown and Gloversville in the Progressive cause. Roosevelt made speeches arguing that America should enter the ongoing world war.

Republican Charles Whitman defeated the Progressive Party's Davenport and other candidates in the gubernatorial election that year. Davenport later returned to the Republican Party and was elected to the state senate and Congress.

UNFORTUNATE COINCIDENCE

Douglas Robinson, Theodore Roosevelt's brother-in-law, died at Amsterdam City Hospital on September 12, 1918. Robinson was traveling with his wife,

Corinne, on a New York Central train bound from New York City to their country home in Warren, Herkimer County. Robinson had acute indigestion on the train, and a doctor on board encouraged the couple to get off in Amsterdam for medical treatment. Robinson died at the hospital that night. Corinne Roosevelt Robinson was the former president's younger sister. She was a poet, writer and lecturer and an aunt of Eleanor Roosevelt.

When Theodore Roosevelt died in January 1919 at age sixty, all business in Amsterdam was suspended for a brief period during the funeral. Local memorial services were held at the Second Presbyterian and First Methodist Churches later that week. There was a memorial service at the Rialto Theater in February. The Theodore Roosevelt memorial flag reached Amsterdam from the west in September. And in late October, there was "Roosevelt Day." Clergymen of the city paid tribute to the "great statesman."

When Amsterdam built a junior high school on Guy Park Avenue in 1925, it was named for Theodore Roosevelt. Former student Paul Russo remembered that longtime junior high principal Fritz Heil told students that he had met Roosevelt: "He said that when he was a kid, Teddy Roosevelt came to town and Heil jumped up on the running board of Roosevelt's car and shook hands with him."

The junior high was demolished after the 1977 moving up ceremony. The Theodore Roosevelt Senior Apartments were built on the site.

JACK RUBY'S ROOMMATE
A GLOVERSVILLE NATIVE

George Senator, who was born in Gloversville, was living with Jack Ruby on November 24, 1963. That day, Ruby, a Dallas nightclub operator, left their apartment. He ended up in the basement of police headquarters, where he shot and killed Lee Harvey Oswald. Oswald was in police custody, held for the assassination two days earlier of President John F. Kennedy.

The FBI interviewed Senator in December 1963. Attorneys Burt W. Griffin and Leon D. Hubert Jr., from the Warren Commission, headed by Supreme Court justice Earl Warren, interviewed Senator for two days in April 1964. When the marathon deposition was at an end, Senator said he feared his life had been forever altered.

> *Mr. GRIFFIN: Now that you raise that, we might get on the record the fact that I believe you have expressed to me at lunch during the last 2 days that you feel that this is an unfortunate circumstance in your life.*
>
> *Mr. SENATOR: Certainly it is. It ain't going to do my life any good.*
>
> *Mr. GRIFFIN: Would you explain? Would you want to convey some of the feelings here on the record that you gave to me?*
>
> *Mr. SENATOR: I feel I will always be pointed at, if anybody knows my name of the nature of the conditions that surrounds me.*
>
> *Mr. GRIFFIN: You feel a certain amount of shame or disgrace?*
>
> *Mr. SENATOR: No; let me say there will probably be a disturbance. They will always point to Jack Ruby's roommate, Jack Ruby's roommate, something of that nature, you know.*

Gloversville native George Senator was photographed at the Dallas apartment he shared with Jack Ruby after Ruby killed JFK assassination suspect Lee Harvey Oswald. *Sixth Floor Museum at Dealey Plaza.*

George Senator was born in Gloversville in 1913, the son of Abraham and Anna Senator. He told the Warren Commission he left school after the eighth grade. In 1929, he moved to the Bronx, where he lived with his sister, Freda Weisberg, and was employed by a company that provided silk for women's dresses.

LOST LINKS TO FAMOUS PEOPLE

In 1932, he returned to Gloversville because he had developed lung trouble. While at home, he worked at a restaurant called Senator's owned by his brother Jacob. The restaurant was at 56 North Main Street and later at 8 Church Street.

In the late 1930s, George Senator moved back to the Bronx and got a job as a soda jerk. He spent one winter doing similar work in Florida.

In August 1941, Senator enlisted in the U.S. Army. He served as an aerial armorer with the Fifth Air Force in the Australian and Pacific Theater during World War II and was honorably discharged in 1945. Jacob Senator told the *Leader Herald* in 1963 that his brother George contracted malaria during the war.

After the war, George Senator and another man operated Denise Foods, a luncheonette in New York City. He married a woman named Shirley Baren in 1946, and they had a son named Bobby in 1947. George and Shirley divorced in 1956 but had lived separately for several years before that. Their son lived with his mother, who later married a man named Milton Wechsler.

Senator worked for a restaurant in Miami and later sold women's wear in Florida for a firm based in Chicago. The company sent him to Dallas in 1954.

In Dallas, Senator sold women's wear but also tried other jobs, including sales of picture postcards. And he started doing work for nightclub and strip club owner Jack Ruby. Ruby and Senator had met at a nightclub. Born Jacob Leon Rubenstein in a tough neighborhood in Chicago, Ruby shortened his name after moving to Dallas.

When Senator was unemployed in 1962, Ruby took him in. They shared an apartment for about five months. Senator moved out when he found work and also found another roommate. Ruby then moved to the same apartment building, 223 South Ewing. Senator had trouble making the rent again when his new roommate, Stanton Corbat, got married and moved out. Senator again moved in with Ruby the first week of November 1963.

Senator told the Warren Commission that Ruby was happy to hear that President Kennedy was coming to Dallas. According to the Warren Commission transcript, the conversation was as follows:

> *Mr. HUBERT. Did Jack tell you why he felt happy about it?*
> *Mr. SENATOR. No; I just don't remember if he did relate that or not, but we thought it was a great honor for him to come to Dallas.*

Senator said Ruby closed his Carousel Club for the weekend after the death of the president: "He thought it was a terrible thing for anybody to be dancing and entertaining or drinking of that nature there at a time such as this."

Sunday morning, Senator said, Ruby received a call from Karen Carlin, one of the dancers at his club, who needed money. According to Senator, Ruby left the apartment about 11:00 a.m. Sunday for two reasons: to pick up receipts from the Carousel Club and to wire money to the dancer, who was now in Fort Worth.

Ruby took his gun, which Senator said Ruby usually did when he was retrieving money from the club. He also put his dog Sheba in the car. Some report Ruby had two pet dogs in his car.

Senator told investigators Ruby would not have taken his beloved dog if he had planned to kill Oswald.

> *Mr. GRIFFIN: Let me ask you this: After you heard that Jack had killed Oswald, did you have any idea, did you think, why did he do it?*
> *Mr. SENATOR: I hadn't the slightest idea. I couldn't imagine why. I'll tell you why I say that. Because he never at any time ever gave me any indication of anything.*

Senator said he believed Ruby came up with the idea of shooting Oswald on the spur of the moment and said he did not think Ruby was involved in any "subversive organizations."

Some assassination websites, however, state that Senator did tell Warren Commission investigator Arlen Specter, who went on to serve in the U.S. Senate, that before leaving the apartment, Ruby did say he planned to kill Oswald.

Ruby was at Dallas police headquarters when Oswald was being escorted to a car for transport to the county jail. Ruby stepped out of a crowd to shoot and fatally wound Oswald. The shooting was broadcast live on national television. Senator heard what had happened while having breakfast at the Eatwell Restaurant.

> *Mr. SENATOR: Now, this is the place that I go every morning, you know, rather Sunday or Monday because I don't like to sit indoors. So I went there and had a cup of coffee. Then the first thing—then I had another cup of coffee. Now, on my second cup of coffee I heard the girl, the waitress—now where she got her information from I don't know. It had to be either telephone or radio, I don't know which. Maybe they had the radio on.*

LOST LINKS TO FAMOUS PEOPLE

Mr. HUBERT: Did you notice any kind of a radio of any type in the restaurant?

Mr. SENATOR: No.

Mr. HUBERT: Did they usually have any?

Mr. SENATOR: Not to my knowledge.

Mr. HUBERT: All right, what happened?

Mr. SENATOR: Not to my knowledge. The first time she said she heard that somebody shot Oswald.

Mr. HUBERT: Was she speaking to you?

Mr. SENATOR: No; no, it was loud; but it happened to be she was near me.

Mr. HUBERT: There were other people in the place?

Mr. SENATOR: Not a lot. There were others you know, the usual morning Sunday business in the restaurant is sort of minute. So what I did when I heard that, I called up the lawyer. I was going to give him the news. I figured he would probably be sitting home, you know, Jim Martin, who happens to be a friend of mine. But when I called him, I spoke to his daughter, and she told me her dad and mother were in church. Dad would be home in half an hour. I said all right, maybe I'll call him back. A short while later, the same girl, the same waitress hollered out that the man—she wasn't pronouncing the name right, the Carousel Club, but I sort of got the drift of the name and she hollered Jack Ruby killed Oswald. This is what she come up with later.

Mr. HUBERT: How much later?

Mr. SENATOR: I would probably say about five minutes.

Mr. HUBERT: But it was after you had called Martin?

Mr. SENATOR: Yes; after I called Martin.

Mr. HUBERT: You called Martin right away?

Mr. SENATOR: Yes; I was going to tell him that. I didn't think he would be—of course, I didn't know he was going to church or anything.

Mr. HUBERT: He is a close friend of yours?

Mr. SENATOR: Yes. He is an attorney there; yes.

Mr. HUBERT: All right, then?

Mr. SENATOR: Then when I heard that again, then I went up to see [Martin].

Senator met that night in his apartment with his friend and lawyer Martin; Ruby's lawyer, Tom Howard; and two journalists, Bill Hunter and Jim Koethe. Three of the men who attended that meeting died within sixteen months. Howard apparently died of a heart attack. Hunter was reported shot accidentally by a police officer when the officer dropped his gun. Koethe was killed by a karate chop from an intruder in his apartment, and the murderer was not indicted.

Senator told the Warren Commission he was scared for about ten days after Oswald was killed: "In other words, for about ten days I was afraid to sleep in the same place twice. Who I was to fear I don't know, but just the normal thing, I was afraid."

Senator told investigators that Ruby was not gay. Ruby did not smoke and drank only occasionally, said Senator, and Ruby was disturbed because he thought Senator consumed too much alcohol. He said Ruby observed all the important Jewish holidays.

Senator was a defense witness at Ruby's trial in 1964. Ruby was sentenced to death but appealed the conviction. He died from pneumonia and lung cancer in 1967 while awaiting a new trial.

Jacob Senator, George's brother, died in Gloversville in 1969, and George Senator was listed in his brother's obituary as living in Las Vegas. George Senator died in the spring of 1992, according to David Reitzes of the Spartacus Educational website.

THE MOHAWK VALLEY TRIP BOBBY KENNEDY NEVER MADE

New York senator and presidential candidate Robert F. Kennedy had been expected in Amsterdam on June 6, 1968. However, that was the day Kennedy died in California.

City resident Sam Vomero recalled that a sign announcing the date of the pending visit had been posted in the window of Kennedy's campaign headquarters, the vacant Crown cigar store on East Main Street, a few doors west of Church Street.

Assassin Sirhan Sirhan shot Kennedy early on the morning of June 5 as the presidential candidate was being escorted through the crowded kitchen pantry of the Ambassador Hotel in Los Angeles. Kennedy had just announced his victory in the California Democratic primary. He died of his injuries the next day.

Kennedy's last words to the crowd in California had been, "And it's on to Chicago [where the Democratic convention would be held] and let's win there."

Kennedy was scheduled to head back for a campaign trip in New York right after the California primary. A *Recorder* editorial on June 6 stated, "Plans had called for Senator Kennedy to be in Amsterdam later this week to open his Presidential campaign headquarters."

A memorial service for Senator Kennedy was held on June 9 at Amsterdam's Lynch High School. The speaker was Robert Lincoln Hatch, head of the school's Social Studies Department and a native of Boston who spoke with an accent reminiscent of the Kennedys.

Robert F. Kennedy with his wife, Ethel, addressing a crowd at the Ambassador Hotel in Los Angeles while claiming victory in the 1968 California presidential primary. Kennedy was assassinated by Sirhan Sirhan after leaving the ballroom. *JFK Presidential Library.*

"During the last few months of his life," Hatch said, "Robert Kennedy traveled from the burned-out villages of South Vietnam to the hungry in Appalachia, from the slums of New York City to the migrant labor camps in California. He had great feeling for these people."

HAPPIER DAYS

Bobby Kennedy had visited Amsterdam on September 17, 1960, when his brother Jack was running for president. The younger Kennedy, then thirty-four, addressed a fundraiser for the Montgomery County Democratic Committee at St. John's Hall, now the Elks Lodge.

LOST LINKS TO FAMOUS PEOPLE

Bobby Kennedy also came to Amsterdam on October 19, 1964, during his campaign for U.S. Senate. Kennedy defeated one-term Republican senator Kenneth Keating in a national sweep for Democrats the year after President Kennedy was killed.

In his Amsterdam visit, Kennedy first stopped at Democratic headquarters in the former Enterprise Store on East Main Street. Hugh Donlon reported in the *Recorder* that "great numbers" wanted to shake hands with the candidate.

Kennedy then held a rally in the same Grove Street parking lot his brother had used in 1960 when campaigning for president. The elder brother drew a crowd of 3,000 while an estimated 1,200 were on hand to hear Bobby. Skies were cloudy in 1964, and the event was threatened by rain.

There was what Donlon called "a juvenile outburst" as the candidate was about to speak. Kennedy got the crowd laughing as he said, "Senator Keating doesn't like to read about yelling so please keep your voice down. However, it's all right with me."

Congressman Sam Stratton told the crowd Kennedy would carry Amsterdam by a wide margin. The candidate was introduced by county commissioner of welfare Sasen Hage.

After leaving Amsterdam, Kennedy stopped at Canajoharie, where he shook hands with millworkers. Over one hundred students were excused from study halls to attend. One heckler made remarks on the carpetbagger issue; Kennedy was a Massachusetts resident living in Virginia when he announced his New York U.S. Senate run.

The candidate then stopped at the Kennedy Road, St. Johnsville farm of Stanley and Melanie Shuster, who later received a letter of appreciation from the candidate. The Little Falls newspaper estimated the crowd in St. Johnsville at four hundred.

Christine Oarr Eggleston was in school at the time in St. Johnsville. "As I recall, everyone just took off from school (including my brother, Brian Oarr) to head on up there to hear what RFK had to say. I asked my brother later what was said but all I remember him telling me was that RFK handed out licorice in the shape of a pipe."

Kennedy then traveled to Little Falls, where he was met by an "enthusiastic throng" and ended the day with a dinner at Syracuse University.

Kennedy won the 1964 Senate election by 700,000 votes statewide and took Montgomery County by 3,000 votes. President Johnson that year took New York by 2.6 million votes and won Montgomery County over Barry Goldwater by 10,000 votes.

ARTIST FREDERIC REMINGTON MARRIED A GLOVERSVILLE WOMAN

Artist Frederic Sackrider Remington, famous for depicting the American West in paintings and sculptures, married a woman who lived in Gloversville.

Eva Caten was born in Howlett Hill near Syracuse in 1859, went to school in that area and then lived at 85 South Main Street in Gloversville as a young woman. Her father, Lawton Caten, was superintendent of the Fonda, Johnstown & Gloversville Railroad for twenty-three years.

Remington, born in 1861 in Canton, New York, was an indulged only child. His father, Seth Pierrepont Remington, was a Civil War colonel. Eliphalet Remington, who founded the firearms factory in Ilion, was a distant cousin.

Frederic Remington loved the outdoors and physical activity. He had skill in art but was reluctant to take art classes when he attended Yale. He left Yale in 1879 to help care for his father, who died of tuberculosis the next year.

Caten met Remington while on an outing at Cranberry Lake in Canton that year. Historian Jacqueline Murphy wrote, "Frederic fell deeply in love and lost no time in asking for her hand. Frederic's reputation of his inability to hold a job preceded him and Mr. Caten refused. Daunted but determined to make his fortune, Frederic set out for the west."

Eva and Frederic finally married in 1884 in Gloversville. Remington was living in Kansas City at the time. Eva went there but soon left Frederic and returned to Gloversville, discouraged that her husband was half owner of a saloon.

They reconciled within a year, and Remington's career as a magazine and book illustrator took off. Murphy said the turning point was when an illustration of the search for Geronimo appeared under Remington's name in *Harper's Weekly* in 1886. He began to sculpt in 1895. Hearst newspapers sent him to Cuba to sketch the Spanish-American War.

Murphy wrote, "On December 20, 1909, [Remington] went to bed with severe stomach pains. Although he had an emergency appendectomy, he died the day after Christmas. He was 48 years old and at the peak of his career." The artist was extremely overweight, and that may have contributed to his demise.

The Remingtons were living then in Ridgefield, Connecticut. Eva wrote in her diary, "It seems very lonesome without Frederic. The whole house is filled with his presence. Feel as though all had gone from me."

Sue Schrems, who was a history professor at Rose State College in Oklahoma City, said Eva set to work marketing the sketches, paintings and sculptures her husband left behind to provide a steady income. Eva knew she needed to keep alive the public's interest in Remington's work illustrating the West.

In 1915, Eva moved to Ogdensburg in northern New York, near where her husband originally came from. She died there in 1918 and gave many of Remington's western art works to the Ogdensburg library.

Broncho Buster

Remington's 1895 sculpture *Broncho Buster*, also spelled *Bronco Buster*, has been called the most famous piece of American art. An original cast of the statue can be seen during presidential speeches delivered from the Oval Office at the White House.

An eighteen-inch-high casting of *Broncho Buster* was given to Gloversville Public Library by local relatives of Eva Caten Remington in 1919. In 1932, the statue was stolen by someone who had hidden inside the library at closing time.

The thief, named in news accounts as Charles Bell, sold the statue for $100 to an antiques dealer in Woodstock. The statue (identified by a secret marking put on the statue by the library) was located by authorities in New York City and returned to the Gloversville library on East Fulton Street. It

A casting of Frederic Remington's iconic statue *Broncho Buster* is on display at the Gloversville Public Library. Remington's wife, Eva, had lived in Gloversville. *Kathy Snyder.*

is still there on display on the second floor but bolted in place to prevent a reoccurrence of the theft. The Arkell Museum in Canajoharie, New York, also has a casting of *Broncho Buster*.

LOST LINKS TO FAMOUS PEOPLE

Postcard view of Gloversville Public Library from early 1900s. Novelist and Gloversville native Richard Russo credits the library with inspiring his writing career. *Jerry Snyder.*

Built in 1904 with a grant from philanthropist Andrew Carnegie, the Gloversville Public Library embarked on a multimillion-dollar renovation campaign in 2014. Honorary chairman is bestselling novelist and Gloversville native Richard Russo.

Russo told the *New York Times*, "I just have this feeling that if it weren't for the Gloversville Free Library that I probably would not be a writer."

MIKE TYSON DISCOVERED IN PERTH

Amsterdam Editor a Veteran of the Tyson Circus

In 1974, Bobby Stewart won the National Golden Gloves Tournament as a light heavyweight, beating Mike Dokes in Denver, Colorado.

It was the high point of Stewart's amateur boxing career and was preceded by numerous regional bouts. His amateur record was forty-five wins and five losses.

Stewart was raised in Amsterdam on McDonnell Street and Chapel Place. His father was a New York state trooper, and his mother worked in local doctors' offices. For many years, Stewart has lived in Tribes Hill, between Amsterdam and Fonda.

Stewart turned professional after the 1974 Golden Gloves and won thirteen of his sixteen fights. But he was disturbed by what he felt was an unfair decision in one of the professional fights. He regrets that he did not wait to compete in the 1976 Olympics before embarking on his professional boxing career.

By 1976, Stewart was working as a counselor at the now closed Tryon School for young men in trouble with the law in Perth in Fulton County. Over the years, he also tended bar at Russo's Tavern in Amsterdam and the Chelsea House in Tribes Hill.

Mike Tyson, a street tough from Brooklyn, became one of the inmates at Tryon in the late 1970s. Tyson wanted to learn boxing techniques and wanted Stewart to train him. Tyson even acted up so he could get transferred to Elmwood, the residents' cottage with the toughest young men, where Stewart was assigned.

LOST LINKS TO FAMOUS PEOPLE

Stewart said Tyson was "looking to do something, either bad or good." Under Stewart's strict regimen, Tyson, not yet a teenager, began to improve in fighting skills and academic subjects. The young man's reading went from third-grade to seventh-grade level. Stewart still bristles that Tyson was labeled "borderline retarded" at the reform school.

Stewart said, "He was a complete gentleman as he wanted to fight so bad." He was observed by staff practicing boxing routines in his room at 1:45 a.m.

"A good work ethic is very important," Stewart said. And Tyson was willing to work. As Tyson progressed, he became stronger, breaking Stewart's nose in one sparring session. Fortunately, the older fighter had the next week off from Tryon and was able to recuperate and continue training Tyson. Stewart did not tell Tyson about the broken nose until years later.

After a few months, Stewart got permission to take Tyson for a day to Catskill, New York, where the young boxer's skills could be assessed by trainer Constantine "Cus" D'Amato. Stewart knew D'Amato, who had worked with champion boxers including Floyd Patterson and Jose Torres.

Stewart and Tyson were boxing three rounds for D'Amato and gym manager Teddy Atlas. Stewart hit Tyson in the nose toward the end of the three-round match, and the young man began bleeding although his nose was not broken.

Atlas wanted to stop the fight, but Tyson said he wanted to finish it, as he always did three rounds with Stewart. They finished the three rounds.

D'Amato pronounced that barring outside distractions, Tyson, then twelve or thirteen, would become world heavyweight champion.

D'Amato adopted the young fighter after Tyson's mother died. Tyson did become a champion in 1986 shortly after D'Amato died. But the boxer's life since has been marked by a rape conviction, controversies and outrageous acts, including biting off part of an ear of opponent Evander Holyfield in 1997.

Stewart last saw Tyson in 2013, when the former champion had a limousine sent to Amsterdam to take Stewart to Westbury, Long Island, to see Tyson's one-man stage show.

The next morning, Tyson and Stewart met for breakfast and discussed the possibility of jointly doing motivational talks to help students or even prisoners. Stewart, however, has not heard anything since from Tyson on that subject.

LOST MOHAWK VALLEY

THE TYSON CIRCUS

When Mike Tyson rocketed to fame in the 1980s, Paul Antonelli went along for the ride. Antonelli was the reporter whom Tyson and his camp trusted the most.

Antonelli grew up in Coxsackie, earned a political science degree from the University at Albany and considered becoming a lawyer. He covered sports for newspapers instead and became a familiar face to Tyson; Tyson's foster father, Cus D'Amato; and trainer Kevin Rooney. Antonelli married Susan Cally, the daughter of the Catskill doctor who treated D'Amato's boxers. The Callys and Tyson were friends.

Tyson became a huge media sensation, and Antonelli consistently got the inside story. His accounts of Tyson's boxing matches and outrageous actions outside the ring appeared in international media outlets.

"The London papers then paid very well," Antonelli said.

Antonelli was one of five American reporters who traveled to Japan to cover Tyson's 1990 loss to Buster Douglas in Tokyo. Tyson was in prison from 1992 to 1995 on a rape conviction. Antonelli covered other sports beats then—the New York Knicks and New York Giants. He continued to cover Tyson after the boxer's release from jail and was there in 1997 when Tyson bit the ears of his opponent Evander Holyfield.

After that Las Vegas match, Antonelli decided to, as he describes it, "leave the circus." There was gunfire after the second Holyfield fight. Tyson's world had become a dangerous and disheartening place.

In 1998, Antonelli was hired as sports editor of the *Amsterdam Recorder*. Seventeen years later, he's still there. He enjoys covering and editing coverage of high school and other local sports. He and his wife live in Amsterdam, and he is active in the community. He's president of the Amsterdam Youth Baseball League, which has three hundred young members. He also volunteers with Amsterdam Little Giants football. His two sons play basketball and baseball.

He still talks with Tyson from time to time. At one point, Antonelli was collaborating on a book with Tyson trainer Kevin Rooney, but that project fell through. Someday Antonelli hopes to write a book about his years covering Tyson. But for now, he's enjoying his life in Amsterdam.

LOST LINKS TO FAMOUS PEOPLE

BOXING IN AMSTERDAM

According to former *Recorder* columnist George Lazarou, Amsterdam was a boxing mecca in the late 1930s, a legacy of boxing matches arranged for soldiers at the South Side Armory. Lazarou himself was a fighter, trained by Buddy Benoit. Benoit once lost a close contest to the famous Jake Lamotta.

Boxing was so popular in Amsterdam that eight thousand fans attended the city playground championship at Lynch School fields one year in the 1930s. In a bout held behind Lanzi's tavern on the South Side, the press of the crowd collapsed a wooden fence around the arena.

Many of Amsterdam's pugilists then were Italian American. Sammy and Jimmy Pepe, who operated a popular West Main Street restaurant, trained fighters at the Mount Carmel Athletic Club in the basement of the former church building on the South Side. Jo Jo Zeno had training quarters at his Ringside Athletic Club on East Main Street.

Zeno trained John Duchessi Sr. and his older brother Peter. John Duchessi Sr.—father of the former mayor John Duchessi Jr.—said boxers earned two dollars a fight.

Duchessi Sr. fought in one of the earliest televised bouts in 1942, broadcast by General Electric's WRGB from the basement of the television station

In 1938, Sam Pepe moved his popular restaurant to 218 West Main Street, and it continued to be a gathering place for Amsterdam boxers. *Wm. J. Kline & Son*, Amsterdam Recorder, *Walter Martin, Mark Perfetti.*

building then adjacent to the entrance to the Scotia bridge in Schenectady. Duchessi slugged his way to a decision over Don Trott of Saratoga Springs. Amsterdam's Tony Marcellino defeated Mal Johnson of Albany in another televised match that night.

Many local fighters, including Duchessi, went off to fight in World War II, and the local boxing scene never recovered. Television also brought national fights into the homes of boxing fans.

"Nobody wanted to get punched for two dollars after the war," Duchessi said.

CHAMPION BOXER GENE TUNNEY TRAINED IN SPECULATOR

World heavyweight champion James Joseph "Gene" Tunney trained for his most important fights in Speculator in the Adirondacks in the 1920s. Speculator is a village in the town of Lake Pleasant in Hamilton County.

Born in New York City in 1897, Tunney was one of seven children of a poor Irish immigrant family. "In the home of my rearing, prayer was regular and fervent," Tunney said.

He joined the U.S. Marines in World War I and fought in the ring rather than in the trenches, becoming boxing champion of the U.S. Expeditionary Forces.

Tunney met William Osborne from Speculator in the marines, and Osborne invited Tunney to come to Speculator and establish a training camp. The Osbornes owned two hotels and tourist cabins in the Adirondack village.

In 1926, Tunney trained in Speculator for his first world heavyweight championship fight against Jack Dempsey. Tunney won the fight in a ten-round decision. Osborne publicized Tunney's training camp and got tourists to come, boosting Speculator's economy.

Tunney trained in Speculator for his 1927 rematch with Dempsey. Tunney won that fight in a unanimous decision despite the controversial "long count." Dempsey knocked Tunney down in the seventh round, but the referee did not start the count on Tunney for several seconds as Dempsey did not immediately go to a neutral corner. The two boxers later became good friends.

Boxer Gene Tunney trained in Speculator in the Adirondacks during the 1920s. *Hamilton County historian Eliza Darling.*

Tunney trained in Speculator in 1928 for one more fight as world champion, defeating Tom Heeney of New Zealand. Tunney then resigned from boxing, apparently a promise made to Mary "Polly" Lauder, the wealthy socialite he married that year.

Other fighters—including Max Baer, his brother Buddy Baer, Max Schmeling, Maxie Rosenbloom, Jim Slattery and Knute Hansen—also trained in Speculator, according to a pamphlet prepared by Lake Pleasant seventh graders in 1986 under the supervision of former town historian Ernest D. Virgil.

The fighters who came in later years were more ostentatious than Tunney. Max Baer for one was said to love attention.

Famous people came to see the boxers train. According to the student report, "Bernard Gimbel of Gimbel's [department store] in New York suffered a few bruises when his plane, leaving the golf course in Lake Pleasant, failed to climb high enough to miss the trees at the end of the fairway."

After retiring from boxing, Tunney wrote a book (*A Man Must Fight*) and then went into business. He reenlisted in the military in World War II and was a lieutenant commander in the U.S. Navy, heading the navy physical fitness program. He died in 1978.

GENE TUNNEY PARK

One of the champion's sons, Jay R. Tunney of Chicago, has written a book called *The Prizefighter and the Playwright* about the seemingly improbable friendship between his father and playwright George Bernard Shaw, who was a boxing fan.

Donations totaling over $200,000 were made to create Gene Tunney Park just off Route 30 in Speculator. The park is at the site formerly occupied by one of the Osborne hotels.

Jay Tunney holds a plaque honoring his father, Gene Tunney, at the 2014 dedication of Gene Tunney Park in Speculator. *Barbara Schoonmaker.*

LOST MOHAWK VALLEY

Jay Tunney and his wife, Kelly, joined well over one hundred people for dedication ceremonies on August 28, 2014. Also on hand were Speculator mayor Letty Rudes and Town of Lake Pleasant supervisor Neil McGovern.

Jay Tunney told the *Daily Gazette*, "[My father] was undistracted in Speculator. That was the best part. He could think of things and clear his mind and have things the way he wanted."

When Gene Tunney was not training, he was frequently found reading. His son said his father's favorite saint was St. Francis, and the calm and beauty of the Adirondacks were helpful to him.

Another son of Gene Tunney, John V. Tunney, served in the U.S. House of Representatives for six years and was a one-term United States senator from California.

SHOW BUSINESS SIBLINGS RETIRED TO GLOVERSVILLE AREA

The Glorias were a popular European-born sister-and-brother dancing team who spent their later years in Gloversville and Caroga Lake.

Doing research for a book on a flamboyant costume designer (*Madame Sherri: The Special Edition*), historian David Fiske came across the story of Adelaide Gloria Hollenbeck and her brother, Albert Gloria. Madame Sherri designed elaborate costumes worn by the Glorias.

Adelaide and Albert's parents—Count Adolphe Deneveloff, a Russian, and Anna Wagner, a German said to be descended from Richard Wagner—were European lion tamers who had pronounced their wedding vows inside a lion cage as a publicity stunt. Wagner performed as Anna Gloria with the Barnum and Bailey Circus.

Adelaide was born in Normandy, France, and Albert was born in London. The siblings began dancing as toddlers in Europe. Showman Florenz Ziegfeld said Adelaide had "the most beautiful legs in the world." According to critic Dorothy Parker, Ziegfeld apparently paid that compliment to more than one woman.

The Glorias' father died, and Adelaide, Albert and mother Anna came to the United States in 1913 and lived in Bayside, Queens. The brother-and-sister team performed in cabaret shows and restaurant revues in the New York City area and toured on vaudeville's Keith circuit. Adelaide and Albert specialized in dancing that imitated ice-skating and roller-skating.

Albert and Adelaide Gloria playing Casparoni and Mrs. Casparoni in George M. Cohan's musical *The Rise of Rosie O'Reilly* in 1923. *New York State Museum.*

The Glorias, who earned as much as $5,000 a week, were acquainted with celebrities, including Bing Crosby, W.C. Fields and Vernon and Irene Castle.

In 1923, they were cast as Casparoni and Mrs. Casparoni in George M. Cohan's musical *The Rise of Rosie O'Reilly*. The play debuted before packed houses in Boston and ran for three months in New York. Dancer Ruby Keeler had her debut in the play.

LOST LINKS TO FAMOUS PEOPLE

TROUBLE ON LONG ISLAND

In 1933, Adelaide claimed that she had been attacked by admirer and Cuban businessman Francis Xiques at a Long Island hotel. Xiques denied the charge, but later that year, Adelaide was chloroformed and beaten while walking home from a friend's house.

Fiske said it was suspected that this attack was connected to the pending lawsuit Adelaide had against Xiques. The legal dispute was resolved with a deal involving a cash settlement, although Xiques apparently did not pay up.

In 1940, brother and sister retired from show business. Albert got a job with Republic Aircraft Corporation on Long Island.

In 1942, Adelaide married Sidney F. Hollenbeck of Gloversville, a native of Mayfield. Hollenbeck was introduced to Adelaide by a movie actress friend, Marguerite Gale, a native of the town of Glen in the Mohawk Valley. Between 1915 and 1919, Gale performed in *Molly Malone Made Good*, *The Yellow Menace* and *Mandarin's Gold*. According to a movie website, Gale died in Amsterdam in 1948.

Adelaide, sometimes known as Adele, and Sidney lived at 12 Clinton Street in Gloversville and later moved to Caroga. In 1956, Sidney took his own life, shooting himself twice with a shotgun at the couple's home on the Gloversville–Caroga Lake Road. The *Leader Herald* reported that he had been despondent for several months. He was working at G. Levor & Company, a leather-tanning mill in Gloversville.

Adelaide later took up a hobby, according to a *Leader Herald* story—creating artistic montages from pieces clipped from greeting cards she'd received. In 1960, according to Fiske, her brother, Albert, retired from the airplane company and came to live with her.

Also in 1960, Adelaide was quoted in an Associated Press story recalling a 1919 strike that shut down the New York City theater scene.

Fiske said Adelaide and Albert took numerous trips together. A *Leader Herald* article in 1963 described plans to take their trailer to Florida, California and Guatemala for an extended vacation.

"When you are not active, you are dead," Albert said. Albert died in 1975, and Adelaide passed away in 1982. Gloversville is listed as the last place of residence for both of them.

Part III
LOST PLACES

AMSTERDAM'S ROCKTON

The Lost Ward

In 2014, Historic Amsterdam League conducted tours of Rockton, a section of north Amsterdam with a rich recreational, industrial and residential history.

Tours started at Shuttleworth Park, the summer home of the Amsterdam Mohawks baseball team. The recreational area began as Crescent Park, built by Edward and Thomas McCaffrey in 1914.

The facility was renamed Jollyland when taken over by Fred J. Collins in 1923. Mohawk Carpet Mills started using Jollyland for employee events in 1927. The park was renamed Mohawk Mills Park in 1934, when the carpet mill started operating the facility. In 1939, the park became the home of the Amsterdam Rugmakers, a New York Yankees farm team. The Yankees played twice at the park in the 1940s, and minor-league baseball lasted there into the 1950s.

As the carpet mills began moving out of town, the City of Amsterdam took over Mohawk Mills Park in 1964. The popular Arthur J. Hartig became caretaker in 1966. Hartig's family lived in a white house at the facility. The park was renamed Herbert Shuttleworth II Park in 1977 to honor the last president of Mohawk/Mohasco Carpet who lived in Amsterdam. Hartig retired as park caretaker in 1981.

Crescent Park was created in 1914 in Amsterdam's Rockton section. It was later known as Jollyland, Mohawk Mills Park and today is Herbert Shuttleworth II Park. *Jerry Snyder.*

INDUSTRIAL AND RESIDENTIAL

Mohawk Carpet Mills was created with the 1920 combination of the Shuttleworth family's mill along the Mohawk River—the Lower Mill—and the McCleary, Wallin and Crouse rug factory on Lyon Street and Forest Avenue in Rockton. That complex—started by some of Stephen Sanford's former employees—was known as the Upper Mill.

The last carpet mill facility in Amsterdam closed in 1987. In 1992 and 1994, arson fires gutted the former Upper Mill. Most of the damaged buildings have been torn down.

Originally called Rock City, Rockton was an independent village settled in the late 1700s or early 1800s. Historic Amsterdam League president Jerry Snyder said, "The name came from the rock quarries and lime kilns being operated there."

The name of the village was changed to Rockton in the late 1880s, and the village was annexed by the City of Amsterdam in 1901.

In 1908, Rockton was growing, according to a board of trade manual. Carpet mill executive William McCleary and other influential citizens founded the Rockton Realty Company to develop "a large addition to the city."

A solitary mill building remains in this 2014 picture of the former Upper Mill factory complex in Amsterdam's Rockton section. Many buildings were destroyed in arson fires in the 1990s. *Jerry Snyder.*

Forest Avenue in Amsterdam's Rockton section in the early 1900s. *Jerry Snyder.*

The development was in walking distance of the carpet mill then headed by McCleary on Lyon Street and Forest Avenue. Building lots on new streets off Clizbe Avenue were put up for sale. The streets were named for prominent figures in the carpet industry—Sanford, McCleary, McNeir, Cochrane, Sloane, Clark, Bigelow and Law.

Rockton became Amsterdam's eighth ward. As the city population declined during the course of the twentieth century, the number of wards in the city decreased from eight to five with Rockton split between the first and second wards. The league subtitled its 2014 tour as "The Search for the Lost Ward."

THE ROCKTON WYE

The Rockton Wye is the intersection of Clizbe Avenue, Lyon Street, Hewitt Street and Northern Boulevard. A "wye" in railroad terms is a track configuration resembling a triangle with each point leading to a different route. The trolley routes that crisscrossed Amsterdam and Hagaman met at the Rockton Wye.

The electric trolley car came to the Carpet City with the Amsterdam Street Railway Company in 1890. By 1901, the line had expanded to Rockton, and some pictures show trolleys with the name Amsterdam & Rockton Street Railway. In 1902, the line was extended to Hagaman. Also in 1902, the Amsterdam trolley company was acquired by the Fonda, Johnstown & Gloversville Railroad (FJ&G).

In 1911, the three-way intersection known as the Rockton Wye was built to connect the FJ&G trolley lines that went from the Rockton Wye to Hagaman, Vrooman Avenue in Amsterdam's East End and Market Street in the city's downtown.

Railroad historian and Amtrak engineer Paul Larner wrote:

> *The track configuration at* [the Rockton Wye] *permitted the trolleys to run direct to and from Hagaman via either the original line up Market Street Hill or via Vrooman Avenue and also, by a connecting track, directly around the city, hence the term "belt" line.*
>
> *Stockholders of the railroad had interests in electric power, real estate and industry besides providing local transportation. Trolleys ran both directions around the "belt" offering the new residents of that area a convenient means of getting to Main Street, their employment, local recreation areas and the world via the New York Central Railroad. As an aside, those new homes in Rockton would use electricity generated by a company in which the president of the FJ&G had a principal interest.*

LOST PLACES

Three Fonda, Johnstown & Gloversville trolley cars approaching from different directions at Amsterdam's Rockton Wye. *Jerry Snyder.*

Larner said there were problems with trolley cars that had to climb the severe grade on Amsterdam's Vrooman Avenue:

One was never quite sure when the car wouldn't be able to make the turn at East Main Street descending, or, equally as dangerous, when the car wouldn't be able to get up the hill, sliding back to East Main. Men were employed by the railroad to place sand on the rails when conditions required additional traction. As an additional safety measure, the cars were equipped with magnetic brakes.

The Vrooman Avenue line was abandoned in 1928. All FJ&G electric trolley service ended in 1938, supplanted by bus transportation.

Larner said of the Rockton Wye, "Created as a function of providing trolley transportation for the growing city, it is interesting that the term is being carried on. The rails embedded in the ground at the location of the wye, the bridge abutments across the creek are reminders of the early days in Amsterdam when you could hop on a trolley and travel to find your future."

Larner, a native of Gloversville, is author of *Our Railroad: The History of the Fonda, Johnstown & Gloversville Railroad (1867–1893)*.

REMEMBERING THE GOOD OLD DAYS

Rockton natives in the late twentieth century formed an association to reminisce about the old days. Rockton had its own taverns, restaurants, markets, auto repair shops and candy stores. Ann Firth Torgusen said her father, William David Firth, owned Firth's Finer Foods at 379 Locust Avenue between Lindsay and Ellsworth Streets until the 1970s. Her mother was Nan Ferguson Firth.

Torgusen said Firth's provided finer foods to the executive dining room at Mohawk Carpet and to Herbert Shuttleworth II's home, then on Brookside Avenue.

The family of one-time Eighth Ward alderman John Haas operated a variety store on Lindsay Street and an auto repair garage on Lyon Street, across from the carpet mill. The alderman's son, Sergeant John L. Haas Jr., died in 1943 when his plane went down over Germany.

After World War II, a popular winter activity was ice-skating at Hasenfuss Field on Midline Road just beyond Locust Avenue. The field was named for

A school building on Clizbe Avenue in Rockton that later became part of Collette's manufacturing and other businesses. *Montgomery County Department of History and Archives.*

Forest Avenue Methodist Church in the Rockton section. Today, the Jubilee Fellowship worships there. *Montgomery County Department of History and Archives.*

PFC William E. Hasenfuss Jr., killed at Hickham Field near Pearl Harbor, the first Amsterdam native to die in World War II.

Gail Buchner Breen, who grew up in Rockton, remembers using a scabbard from her skate to hold on to a friend while skating. Scabbards are rubber protectors that fit over the blades of the skates.

"We skated in long chains of kids, frequently snapping the whip, which could be terrifying if you were on the end," Breen said. "The person on the end of the whip frequently landed in a snow bank."

THE CARPET CITY AIRPORT

Local residents say that bootleggers used an airstrip on Route 67 in the town of Amsterdam during Prohibition to fly liquor in from Canada. Sometimes there was a night landing when lighted barrels guided the plane with its alcoholic cargo to a safe touchdown.

The airfield was just outside the city, on the right side of Route 67 when heading toward Saratoga County. The location later became Carl Graziani's auction house.

The field was owned by farmer and aviator George Verkleir, who later became active in the Amsterdam Flying Club, which operated a more substantial airfield near Perth.

Oscar Frisch was the first Perth resident to earn a pilot's license, according to town historian Sylvia Zierak. Frisch's airplane was kept at a field that became the Carpet City Airport, at Hills Corners at the junction of Midline Road and Route 107, the Perth–Galway Road.

The airfield was near the settlement of Perth and often called the Perth Airport, although the land involved is in the town of Broadalbin.

Historian Kenneth Shaw wrote that Art Ruback and Al Wright, both from Amsterdam, began using the Midline Road/Route 107 location as a landing strip in 1936. Wright had learned to fly a biplane at Verkleir's airstrip in the town of Amsterdam.

Real estate records show the Amsterdam Flying Club bought the Midline Road airstrip from Myrtal Eddy in 1939. George Verkleir was one of the principals.

Shaw wrote that the side of a barn was removed to allow storage of two planes: "A 1,500 foot east–west runway was built and later a 2,500 foot north–south runway was added."

The first plane at the field was a Taylor Cub that cost $1,000. The plane was badly damaged when a windstorm blew it into a big hole that had been dug for gasoline tanks. A new tail section had to be installed. The first flying instructor was Ken Young. A large hangar was constructed about 1940, according to Shaw, who said twenty-five airplanes were stored at the airfield.

Sometimes the operation was called the Carpet City Flying Club or Amsterdam Flying Services. The words "Carpet City Airport" were painted on the roof of one of the structures.

In the years leading up to World War II, the government established a Civilian Pilot Training program to teach potential military pilots how to fly. The Carpet City Airport may have been part of that effort.

In September 1941, ten fliers from the local airport flew in formation for a gathering of some forty planes. Taking part in the flight was Gerald E. Snyder, father of local historian Gerald R. Snyder. Gerald E. Snyder learned to fly at Carpet City Airport and owned one-third of an aircraft with two other men.

The local airport prospered right after the war as returning soldiers learned to fly under the GI Bill. But the boom was short-lived, and the airfield was sold to a construction company in 1951.

Real estate records show the airport's hangars, office building, shop and land were sold to American Construction that year.

Fort Johnson native David Noyes wrote that he learned to fly at Carpet City Airport. Noyes was in the Air Scout program of the Boy Scouts in 1947. The curriculum officially included only pre-flight activities, but Noyes and his fellow scouts actually flew planes with local World War II veterans as instructors. The leader of the group was a navy veteran named Leon Smith from Hagaman.

The Scouts had powder blue uniforms and met in Amsterdam for classroom instruction at the Blood Building on Market Street. The Air Scouts had World War II surplus gear at the airport—a fighter plane engine they learned how to take apart and put together, a flight simulator and a miniature jet engine.

"Firing it up was quite impressive," Noyes said. "Pleasant memories, great learning experience."

LOST PLACES

DEMONSTRATION FLIGHT TRAGEDY

During the time when Carpet City Airport was most active, two men died when a two-seater Aeronca plane crashed during a demonstration flight twelve minutes after takeoff on Sunday afternoon, October 6, 1946.

The Aeronca was owned by Ray A. Shaver of 88 Forest Street in Gloversville. Willis E. "Slip" Slater, thirty-three, of 401 Locust Avenue in Amsterdam, was demonstrating the plane to Edward Rytel, twenty, of Perth, who had expressed interest in buying it.

Slater, a longtime pilot and army air corps veteran, was a flying instructor at the airport. He died on impact. Slater's wife, the former Marcella Flaherty, had given birth to their son eight days before the airplane tragedy. Rytel, a wounded veteran and student of aviation, survived about three hours, dying at St. Mary's Hospital. It was not clear who was at the controls at the time of the crash.

THE MOHAWK TEEPEE

Fine Dining in an Amsterdam Rock Quarry

The Mohawk Teepee restaurant was built in the abandoned Ross limestone quarry adjacent to a waterfall off Route 5 in Amsterdam's East End.

The Mohawk Teepee was the brainchild of Myron and Lidia Bazar, both natives of Ukraine. Myron was born in Ternopil and Lidia in Boryslav, according to *Ukrainian Weekly*.

In an oral history interview with the New York State Military Museum, Myron Bazar said he came to Amsterdam at age five, graduated from Amsterdam High School in 1941 and served as an engineer in the U.S. Navy during World War II.

After the war, he worked at General Electric. He and his wife noticed that motels, with easy automobile access, were replacing hotels in Florida. The Bazars built their home and the Mohawk View Motel in the abandoned Amsterdam quarry overlooking Coessens Memorial Park in 1954.

The motel grew, going from an original fifteen units to thirty-six units. In 1961, the Bazars hired local architect William Cooper to design a restaurant for the site. The Bazars were becoming art collectors and collaborated on the design with Cooper, a childhood friend of Myron's.

Cooper's other commissions included Clara S. Bacon Elementary School in Amsterdam, the Montgomery County Office Building in Fonda, Gloversville City Hall and Fire Station and the Florida Town Office Building

Cooper proposed the idea of a tepee for the restaurant, which he translated into an A-frame. Lidia said she had wanted an A-frame all along.

LOST PLACES

The Mohawk Teepee restaurant in Amsterdam's East End set a standard for fine dining from the 1960s through the 1990s. *Historic Amsterdam League: Jerry Snyder.*

The four-hundred-seat restaurant opened in 1962. It featured wooden carvings made by Mohawks and live trees inside. The cocktail lounge was called the Wampum.

Lidia hired waiters from Schenectady's Hotel Van Curler, which was going out of business as the Teepee opened. The first chef previously worked at a private club that had served President Eisenhower.

The next year, Cooper and the Bazars designed an expansion that made the rock wall of the quarry the back wall of the restaurant, a difficult engineering feat. The waterfall outside the restaurant was natural but was augmented when the area went through a dry spell.

Weddings and other elegant functions took place at the Teepee. Governor Nelson Rockefeller visited six times. In March 1966, Rockefeller addressed a joint meeting of Rotary, Kiwanis, Lions and the chamber of commerce at the Teepee, pledging support for restoration work at the Erie Canal's Schoharie Crossing site in Fort Hunter.

The Bazars displayed some of their artwork at the restaurant and motel complex starting in 1971. In 1989, fire destroyed a motel building where the

Bazars had living quarters in front of the restaurant. The fire apparently started from disposal of fireplace ashes. The family escaped but artworks were destroyed.

After the fire, the Bazars moved to Saratoga Springs and pursued their art business. Their son, Peter, operated the restaurant and motel; in later years, the venue also was a dance club. The Mohawk Teepee closed in 1993.

Amsterdam native Mike Hastings bought the property in 1999 and, helped by government loans, hired original architect Cooper to restore the restaurant. Renamed the Cliffside, the elegantly refurbished facility opened in 2003 as a dance club and function space. The Amsterdam High School class of 1963 held a fortieth-anniversary reunion event at the Cliffside.

However, financial problems undid the project. The city foreclosed on the Cliffside in 2006, and prominent businessman John Tesiero purchased the property in 2008. Architect Cooper died in 2013. Tesiero hopes to sell or rent the property.

TOM THE BARTENDER

Tom Foster worked as a busboy and then bartender at the Teepee from 1984 until it closed in 1993. Foster, who today is a collector of Amsterdam-area memorabilia and active in historical societies, helped set up banquet rooms for weekend parties as a teenager and worked the parties, carrying trays of food or dirty dishes from and to the kitchen. The Teepee had two floors, and everything went up or down the stairs. There was no elevator.

Foster was trained to be what he called an "old-fashioned" bartender around his eighteenth birthday, not using a shot glass to measure liquor but silently counting as he poured liquor and mixers into the drinks.

Eventually Foster was responsible for ordering liquor, keeping up the bar and training new bartenders. He continued to work during the banquets, recalling that a back banquet room called "the Cave" had a massive circular fireplace "that would make you melt when the fire really got roaring!"

Foster said in the 1980s, the lounge featured a "bar top" piano and an entertainer who played and sang: "Every once in a while a guest would jump up and belt out a tune."

Foster said the appetizers and bar snacks were first rate, including the signature Reuben Balls made with corned beef, sauerkraut, cheese and

DINING FOR 700, overlooking 40-foot natural water-fall. Facilities for all occasions . . . Sixty-six rooms . . . pool . . . air conditioned.

Phone (518) VIctor 2-7400. New York Thruway Exit #27
Route 5   Amsterdam, New York

Promotional postcard for Amsterdam's Mohawk Teepee restaurant. *Author's collection.*

Thousand Island dressing. "The Reuben Balls would be the hit at every cocktail hour for the banquets."

The Teepee's bread rolls and sweet rolls (a version of a cinnamon roll made with mincemeat) were very popular. Foster said patrons would ask for plates of them and take the leftovers home.

Foster enjoyed working for the Bazars. "I really learned a lot of my social/people skills from working there and being around them and that is why I still keep in touch with them to this day. I feel I owe them a lot!"

Foster said, "Once the dance club came about and the banquets started to decline, it was hard to classify [the Mohawk Teepee] as high end. They pretty much stopped the dining room service a couple years before they closed because of the lack of patrons who wanted to dine there. The place really took on a 'bar smell.' No matter how well you cleaned, it still had the stale beer smell after the weekends."

A FORGOTTEN ADIRONDACK SUMMER THEATER

The Tamarack Playhouse

Malcolm Atterbury, who became a well-respected character actor in Hollywood, married an Amsterdam woman and built a summer theater in the Adirondacks in the 1930s.

Atterbury, known as Mac, was born in Philadelphia in 1907. He was the stepson of W.W. Atterbury, who became president of the Pennsylvania Railroad. Apparently, young Atterbury had the financial wherewithal to pursue his theatrical dreams.

Mac Atterbury met Ellen Hardies of Amsterdam when both were attending the Hilda Spong Theater School in New York City. Hardies had gone to Smith College, found it boring and transferred to the acting school. She was the daughter of Amsterdam district attorney and judge Charles Hardies. Her brother, Charles Hardies Jr., became Montgomery County district attorney in the 1970s.

Atterbury and Hardies married in 1937. Atterbury told an interviewer, "Ellen's parents and some friends were going on a cruise to the West Indies. At ten o'clock in the morning, we decided to get married and go with them for our honeymoon."

Ellen had spent summers as a child at her family's camp in Lake Pleasant. In 1937, she and Mac vacationed there and decided to build a summer theater, which opened in 1938. The theater was west of Lake Pleasant on the Piseco Road. The next summer, the Atterburys created the Tamarack Club, which offered dining and dancing, near the theater.

The Tamarack Playhouse in Lake Pleasant in the Adirondacks in 1938. Kirk Douglas and Karl Malden performed there. *Hamilton County Historian Eliza Darling.*

After the summer theater closed, the Tamarack Playhouse became the Tamarack Shoppe. In 2014, the building was not in use. *Hamilton County Historian Eliza Darling.*

LOST PLACES

Kirk Douglas came up with his stage name when, as Isadore Danielovitch or Isadore Demsky, the Amsterdam native was a stagehand and actor for two summers at Tamarack Playhouse in the late 1930s. Actor Karl Malden, who had changed his own name from George Sekulovich, was also one of the players at Tamarack and suggested that Danielovitch change his name, too.

In an article for *AARP: The Magazine* in March 2015, Douglas said Malden suggested "Kirk" as a first name. Douglas liked the abrupt sound of the word but did not realize "Kirk" meant church in Scottish.

Douglas wrote, "Still, I think it's more interesting today when actors retain their given names. I would be Izzy Danielovitch in *Spartacus*."

Historian Jacqueline Murphy found that the Atterburys lived on McGibbon Avenue in Amsterdam in the cold-weather months while operating the Tamarack Playhouse in the summer. In January 1941, Mac directed a production of *First Lady* by Katharine Dayton and George Kaufman for Amsterdam Little Theater.

During the fall and winter months, Mac would review New York City plays for the local paper. Douglas debuted on Broadway, and Atterbury wrote about it, according to Robert Going's book on World War II, *Where Do We Find Such Men*.

On November 22, 1941, Mac wrote that Douglas debuted playing a Western Union boy in *Spring Again* starring Grace George: "He has one very short scene with Miss George which is quite funny and, as the second act curtain falls, the audience is in gales of laughter. Now that Kirk has made his start, I hope to see more of him in Broadway shows."

When World War II began, Mac put the Tamarack Playhouse on hold and assembled a troupe of actors who performed for coastal defense forces in America. Ellen was having children: Malcolm Jr., Charles and Jill. The Atterburys reopened Tamarack Playhouse after the war.

In 1947, the Atterburys left Lake Pleasant and bought the Capitol Theater in Albany. They put on plays there from October through May each year and performed in summer stock in Brattleboro, Vermont. The Tamarack Playhouse became a retail establishment called the Tamarack Shoppe. The building is still there but at last report was not occupied.

In 1953, *Knickerbocker News* critic Robert Mack gave a rave review to Ellen and Mac for their seventy-first and last show in Albany, *Joan of Lorraine* by Maxwell Anderson. Ellen played Joan of Arc.

That year, the Atterburys moved to Beverly Hills, California, and both began appearing on television and in movies. Mac's first role was in Jack Webb's 1954 movie *Dragnet*. Also in 1954, Kirk Douglas was surprised to find

Atterbury playing a ranch hand as Douglas starred in the film *Man Without a Star*.

Ellen Atterbury, who performed as Ellen Hardies, was in the 1959 movie *High School Big Shot*, the 1965 movie *Joy in the Morning* and the television series *Wagon Train* in 1957. Both she and her husband acted in theaters on the West Coast.

Mac Atterbury appeared in seventy-five films and three hundred television episodes. He is best remembered for a small role in Alfred Hitchcock's 1959 movie *North by Northwest*. Atterbury plays a weathered rural man dressed in a suit who tells Cary Grant, "That plane's dusting crops where there ain't no crops." The crop-dusting plane then mounts an assault on Cary Grant.

In television, Atterbury performed in five *Perry Mason* episodes, playing the murderer in three of them. He guest-starred on *Gunsmoke*, *The Twilight Zone* and *The Odd Couple*.

Mac Atterbury died in 1992. Ellen Hardies Atterbury died in 1994. Their son Malcolm Jr., a director, teacher and composer, died in 2006.

PEOPLE'S SILK STORE

Once Part of the Fabric of Amsterdam Life

S amuel L. Kupferberg's ancestors were in the fabric trade so it was only logical that he pursued that line of work. Born in Romania in 1893, Sam had seventeen siblings. Two of his older brothers had started fabric businesses in New York City.

Getting to his brothers in America from Codaesti, Romania, was an issue. During World War I, Romanian Jews were confined to their villages. After the war, Sam was allowed to leave the old country in 1920 for New York City, where he worked with his oldest brother, Jacob. Then Sam moved upstate.

According to a newspaper clipping, on October 9, 1926, Sam Kupferberg opened People's Silk Store, which sold fabrics and draperies at 139 East Main Street in Amsterdam. It was described in the ad as "a new store for the people of Amsterdam." The store that previously had been at that location was called the Fashion Silk Store. Kupferberg may have purchased that business, which had gone into bankruptcy.

Sam Kupferberg met Rae Abramson from Schenectady in 1927, and they married that year. The Abramsons owned a bakery on Broadway in Schenectady.

The Kupferbergs lived at first in a flat on Amsterdam's Academy Street. Rae was bookkeeper and a salesperson at the store.

Newspaper ads indicate People's Silk Store moved to 23 East Main Street in March 1927. The store moved back to 139 East Main Street in April 1928. By 1936, the store had made its final move to 117 East Main.

Above: A 1950s winter view of People's Silk Store, Castler's Market and the Mohican Market in downtown Amsterdam. *Audrey Kupferberg.*

Left: Rae and Samuel L. Kupferberg, owners of People's Silk Store. *Audrey Kupferberg.*

LOST PLACES

The Kupferbergs owned that building and the structure next door, which housed the Mohican Market.

In 1933, Sam and Rae adopted Harvey, their first child. Two daughters, Judith and Audrey, were born after World War II.

Although the Kupferbergs sold silk, their daughter Audrey said silk was not her parents' prime product. The store was known for woolens, cottons, satins, taffetas and synthetic fabrics. The store sold draperies, shades, venetian blinds, bedspreads, tablecloths and dress and drapery materials by the yard.

Samuel L. Kupferberg was president for a time of Congregation Sons of Israel and served on its board of directors. He belonged to the Elks and the Masons. At age sixty-three, he died from a heart attack in 1957.

Audrey was eight years old when her father died. "He was a wonderful man, and throughout my youth, people would come up to me in the street and hug me because they remembered how good a man my father was—and I look just like him!"

Rae continued to run the store. Long-term employees were the late Mildred Botaitis and Stella Kibert.

THE FIRE

As millworkers lost their jobs and Amsterdam's downtown declined in the 1960s, the government began purchasing properties, including the Kupferberg building, for urban renewal.

A devastating fire on May 2, 1969, apparently started in the Spanish American Club on the third floor of the People's Silk Store building. Although fire damage was mainly confined to the third floor, People's Silk Store, Mohican Market and J.C. Penney were badly damaged by water and smoke.

A man named Richard Glamm was seriously injured after he stopped his car to help firemen battle the blaze. Glamm fell from the third-floor roof.

In an ad in the *Recorder*, Rae Kupferberg thanked the police and fire departments, the GAVAC ambulance corps and the Salvation Army. She often told her friends, "People's Silk Store went out in a blaze of glory." The buildings involved were demolished starting later that year.

Rae Kupferberg died in 2000; she was ninety-one. Audrey Kupferberg, now a film historian and archivist, and her husband, writer and film critic Rob Edelman, moved to Amsterdam in 1990. They teach film courses at the University at Albany and live in the house on Division Street that Sam and Rae built in 1937.

PEOPLE LOVED LARRABEE'S HARDWARE

John E. Larrabee's hardware store, located on Market Street in downtown Amsterdam for over eighty years, was a beloved institution.

Born in the town of Amsterdam in 1851, Larrabee began his hardware career working for merchant E.T. Leavenworth. In 1876, Larrabee went into partnership with L.L. Dean. Larrabee later partnered with W.G. Barnes in a store that lasted eight years, Larrabee & Barnes.

In 1889, Larrabee married Louise Leavenworth. They had two daughters. When the Sanford Homestead Building was constructed by carpet magnate Stephen Sanford on Market Street in 1890, Larrabee opened his own store in the new building.

The John E. Larrabee Company sold retail and wholesale hardware and provided supplies for area industries. Located at 5 Market Street, the firm expanded and took over 3 Market Street, previously home to the Odd Figure Bazaar.

Larrabee's 1911 obituary said his store had become the most successful hardware business in the city. The paper gave a detailed account of the sixty-year-old merchant's final days: "One week ago Thursday he was out enjoying an automobile ride, but Friday he seemed much weaker. Saturday he was obliged to take to his bed and immediately sank into an unconscious condition, from which he failed to rally." Larrabee had been in poor health for two years. The newspaper cited hardening of the arteries.

Larrabee was succeeded as general manager by his brother-in-law Warner Leavenworth, who died in 1940. Leavenworth's son Thomas, who had joined

LOST PLACES

Right: John E. Larrabee Company hardware store on Market Street in Amsterdam in the 1970s. *Wm. J. Kline & Son, Amsterdam Recorder, Walter Martin, Mark Perfetti.*

Below: Larrabee's sign was visible from Main Street, Route 5 in Amsterdam. *Wm. J. Kline & Son, Amsterdam Recorder, Walter Martin, Mark Perfetti.*

the firm in 1931, became president in 1940. By then, Larrabee's occupied 3–9 Market Street on the east side of a busy downtown thoroughfare.

About 1950, Larrabee's opened its Bargain Barn one mile north of the city at Collins Corners, selling used appliances at low prices. In 1958, William E. Golden of Amsterdam leased the building and operated Golden's Furniture Supermarket at the Collins Corners location.

Larrabee's was sold in 1960, and Tom Leavenworth pursued other business ventures, including his work as treasurer of Amsterdam's Inman Manufacturing, which made machinery for the box-making industry.

The new owners of Larrabee's, Ailing Beardsley and Mary Louise Rossiter, began an expansion of the firm in 1961, putting more emphasis on selling hardware to new industries that were starting in the area as the carpet mills exited. Beardsley and Rossiter hired Samuel H. Anderson as store manager and said they were expanding appliance sales along with Larrabee's previous retail emphasis on hardware, housewares, gifts and toys.

Beardsley and Rossiter apparently were related. A World War II infantry veteran who had operated an industrial supply firm in New Jersey, Beardsley was married to Carol Rossiter. She was originally from Albany, presumably related to Mary Louise Rossiter, who lived in Slingerlands, headed an Albany real estate firm and was treasurer of Livermore Chevrolet.

Beardsley and his family moved to Amsterdam. In 1965, Larrabee's celebrated seventy-five years in business. In 1972, Beardsley's son, also named Ailing, was retail manager of Larrabee's and up for a young business award from the Junior Chamber of Commerce.

As downtown Amsterdam declined, the store closed in the 1970s, but it is not clear exactly when. Historian Jerry Snyder found that the 1973–74 city directory has the "professional plaza" replacing the Sanford building on Market Street. Furs by Gus was at 3 Market, Hays and Wormuth Insurance at 7 Market and there was no listing for 5 Market Street.

LOVING LARRABEE'S

The store was a comforting presence as it adapted to change through the years. An ad from 1886 had Larrabee & Barnes selling stoves, nails, blacksmiths' supplies, saddlery, wheels, horse blankets, halters, collars, whips, guns, gunpowder, hay wire and carpenter tools.

Larrabee's offered Ike Walton fishing boots for $6.95 in March 1937 as over one thousand hunters and fishermen attended the annual Sportsmen's Show in Amsterdam.

In the 1950s, Larrabee's sold toys, especially at Christmas, including Lionel and American Flyer model trains. Each brand installed a model train layout in the store. A 1958 ad offered an American Flyer guided missile train for $33.88 that could fire toy rockets.

LOST PLACES

According to Amsterdam native Emil Suda, former Larrabee's owner Tom Leavenworth and his assistant Nick Canale would travel to the New York City Toy Fair each March to decide what products to stock that Christmas at the popular Amsterdam store.

AMSTERDAM'S BISHOP SCULLY HIGH SCHOOL

When William Aloysius Scully was bishop of Albany, six new Roman Catholic high schools were established in the diocese. The school that opened on a sixty-two-acre lot on upper Church Street in Amsterdam in 1966, three years before Bishop Scully's death, was named in his honor.

St. Mary's Institute on Forbes Street, which dates back to 1881, had been the city's previous Catholic high school. It was adjacent to St. Mary's Church in the heart of the city. Bishop Scully High school was built near the city's outer limits.

The new school was already under construction in February 1966, when three local priests, a banker and other community members packed a hearing to oppose a proposal to change zoning on upper Church Street to permit construction of a bowling alley.

A downtown highway project was in the works that would lead to the demolition of the popular Wil-ton Lanes on West Main Street. Proprietor Tony Griffin proposed a new bowling alley and restaurant at Church Street and Clizbe Avenue, about one thousand feet from school property. The zoning was not changed, the bowling alley was not built and Bishop Scully High School opened in September.

The first principal was Reverend Joseph Oathout. Bishop Scully himself attended formal dedication ceremonies.

There had been a major fundraising campaign to build the school, including a substantial donation from Mohasco carpet company executive Herbert Shuttleworth II.

Bishop William Scully with Amsterdam's Bishop Scully High School in the background. *St. Mary's Institute.*

Students lined up for lunch at Bishop Scully High School. *St. Mary's Institute.*

Scully cheerleaders Tina Ripepi Emanuele and Melanie Marcellino Coman with Yvonne Jordan Piccioca in the background, 1978–79 football season. *St. Mary's Institute.*

The new school was carpeted, according to Reverend Joseph E. Anselment, who was Scully's principal from 1968 through the mid-1970s. Anselment said enrollment and funding were key issues from the start: "I used to do two bingo games a week." Another longtime principal was Sister Ann Tranelli.

There was a small enrollment boost when Gloversville's Catholic high school, Bishop Burke, closed in 1974. Novelist Richard Russo was a Burke honors graduate in 1967.

Scully's first valedictorian was James Edward Going. According to his brother Robert Going, James is retired from a career at Xerox in Rochester.

Among locally well-known alumni is Philip Cortese, now Montgomery County Family Court judge. Cortese started as a freshman when Scully opened in 1966 and recalled that there were rolls of carpet in the building as the interior was not quite ready. Cortese was elected president of the student government. Students organized both an Earth Day march and a debate on the Vietnam War in 1970.

Casper Wells Jr. is a Scully graduate. His son, also named Casper Wells, has played baseball for several major-league teams. Scully

Reverend Joseph Anselment was Bishop Scully principal from 1968 through the mid-1970s. *St. Mary's Institute.*

Sue Roszak was a secretary at Scully. *St. Mary's Institute.*

secretaries included the MLB baseball player's grandmother, Mary Wells. Another well-known secretary was Sue Roszak.

The colorful Francis "Dutch" Howlan coached successful sports teams at Scully until he retired in 1987. The Scully gym was named Howlan Hall in 1982; the coach died in 1989.

Howlan was inducted posthumously into the New York State Basketball Hall of Fame in 2013. Before Scully opened in 1966, Howlan had coached sports teams at St. Mary's Institute during the years the institute was the city's Catholic high school. An alumnus of St. Mary's and a college baseball and basketball standout, Howlan began coaching at St. Mary's in 1953 after the sudden death of athletic director Alex Isabel. Howlan coached twenty-five winning teams that won twenty-seven championships under his leadership.

Francis "Dutch" Howlan, shown here with a champion basketball team, coached many winning athletes. *St. Mary's Institute.*

In a statement on the House floor, Amsterdam congressman Paul Tonko said, "His friends and former players remember him as a dedicated coach, an inspiring mentor and a determined winner. As a fierce competitor, he preached a never-give-up attitude."

Howlan had a lucky pair of bright red socks, given to him by the Scully cheerleaders. After considerable badgering, he reluctantly wore the red socks during a tough game that his team won. He is reported to have worn red socks during games for the rest of his career.

Donna Palczak of Amsterdam first worked at Scully once a week, using what had been the kitchen in the priest's apartment to teach home economics to seven or eight female students.

After a hiatus of some years, Palczak returned to Scully as the librarian. Frugality was the watchword, Palczak said. Money-saving efforts included using both sides of a sheet of paper.

Tuition was rising, enrollment was falling and teachers in religious orders were dwindling. In early May 1990, Bishop Howard Hubbard announced that Scully would close in June. Only eighty-five students had enrolled for the next school year.

Palczak said when the closing was announced at a school assembly, there were tears. And tears returned at the senior prom and at each milestone along the way to the final commencement.

Principal Arlene Maranville told the *Recorder* that the juniors recognized they would not spend their senior year together, "They're upset but they'll be OK."

In December 1990, St. Mary's Institute, a Catholic school for students from early childhood through eighth grade, began moving into the former high school building and remains there today.

Part IV

FORGOTTEN
HISTORY MAKERS

PERTH VALEDICTORIAN'S NAME COULD BE ON THE MOON

Amsterdam's Rocket Man

According to his family, the name of the class of 1938 valedictorian at Perth High School is inscribed on a plaque left on the moon.

Stanley J. Jevitt Sr. was born in Avoca, Pennsylvania, the son of Antoni and Julia Dziewit. The spelling of the family name later was changed to Jevitt. Stanley was the sixth of eight children.

Antoni and Julia were Polish immigrants who originally settled in Amsterdam. They moved to Pennsylvania, where they had a farm and where Antoni worked in the mines. A doctor told Antoni he had early stages of black lung disease and advised him to stop mining. The family returned to the Mohawk Valley and bought a farm on McQueen Road in Perth.

After high school, where he was valedictorian and class president, Stanley Jevitt earned a degree in aeronautical engineering at the University of Alabama. He was the first of his siblings to go to college. Perth school superintendent John Paris said if his parents couldn't afford college, he would see to it that Stanley's bill was paid. One of Jevitt's college classmates was the controversial future Alabama governor George Wallace.

Jevitt learned to fly while in college, graduated in 1942 and enlisted in the U.S. Navy. Stationed in Alameda, California, he was crew chief on the *Martin Mars* flying boat, a huge seaplane that flew supplies between California and Honolulu.

After the war, Jevitt worked at Schenectady General Electric on the development and testing of jet engines. He also operated the Sacandaga

Sea Plane company in Mayfield. He gave flying lessons and transported customers by seaplane on fishing and scenic trips. Jevitt taught his wife, Dorothy, an Indianapolis native; several of their six children; and three of his brothers to fly.

In February 1948, Jevitt survived an airplane accident on snow-covered Mayfield Lake. According to the *Leader Republican*, Jevitt was landing on what he believed was a couple inches of snow on top of the frozen lake. However, there was actually sixteen to eighteen inches of snow cover. The plane nosedived and turned over on landing. No one was injured, but volunteers worked for hours turning the plane upright and towing it off the lake using toboggans.

At GE, Jevitt was an improviser. The company once needed to know how much black powder was required to fire missiles from an airplane and planned to construct a million-dollar building to conduct the test. Jevitt's brother John was in the fireworks business so Jevitt got the job done by testing fireworks without the creation of a costly building.

Jevitt left GE and worked for other aeronautical companies: Bell Aircraft, Lockheed and Martin Marietta. He joined NASA in 1966 at Cape Canaveral in Florida.

In a news release in May 1969, NASA reported that engineer Jevitt was playing a key role in the launch of Apollo 10 that month. The fourth manned mission in the Apollo program, Apollo 10 was a dress rehearsal for the first moon landing.

A Plaque on the Moon?

Jevitt's niece Frances Luzinas said her uncle was included on a list of engineers whose names were inscribed on a plaque left on the moon, most likely during the first moon landing, Apollo 11, in July 1969.

NASA's public information office said there were no official plaques left on the moon with Apollo employee names on them. However, NASA admitted there were unsanctioned actions by employees and contractors that were not formally documented. The NASA statement continued, "Unfortunately, we have no way of confirming whether or not Mr. Jevitt's name was on an unofficial list/plaque."

In later years, Jevitt was assistant to the chief engineer on the space shuttle and contributed to the development of the shuttle's rocket booster.

He died at age seventy-seven on April 18, 1998, at Cape Canaveral Hospital in Cocoa Beach, Florida, and was buried at Arlington National Cemetery.

AMSTERDAM'S ROCKET MAN

Petrone Square, the corner of Church and Main Streets in Amsterdam, is named in honor of Rocco Petrone. Petrone was born in Amsterdam in 1926, the son of Italian immigrants. He was launch director and what the *New York Times* called a "driving force" in the Apollo program.

"Sparsely spoken and self-effacing in public, Petrone was tough, blunt and demanding in private," said Amsterdam city historian Robert von Hasseln. "Once, when a briefing contractor attempted to bluff him on a critical question the contractor could not answer, Petrone physically hustled him off the podium and had him banned from ever working with the space program again."

Petrone's parents came from Sasso di Castalda in Basilicata, Italy. Petrone's father was a railroad laborer killed in a work accident when Rocco was an infant. His mother worked in a glove factory and later remarried.

"As a child, Petrone delivered ice to make family ends meet," von Hasseln said. In World War II, Petrone received an appointment to West Point, where he did well academically and played defensive tackle on the 1945 national championship football team.

He served during the occupation of Germany and later earned advanced degrees at Massachusetts Institute of Technology. He worked on the U.S. missile program in the 1950s and was detailed to the National Aeronautics and Space Administration. He retired as a lieutenant colonel from the army in 1966 to assume the launch director job at NASA.

According to the *New York Times*, Petrone said everything had to be ready at the same time for a successful launch: "Concurrency is the real challenge of this program."

After the moon landing in 1969, Petrone was promoted to direct the entire Apollo program. In 1973, he became director of Marshall Space Flight Center, where he oversaw the Skylab space station project. He retired from NASA in 1975. He became CEO of a resource recovery organization but returned to the space industry as an official of Rockwell International.

Von Hasseln said, "Petrone was one of the few to recommend against the launching of the space shuttle *Challenger* on its last mission in 1986, although his concern was that cold weather would damage its insulating tiles, not the o-ring seals in the booster rockets which failed causing the explosion that destroyed the craft and killed its crew."

Petrone died in 2006 at his home in California. Von Hasseln said, "The day he died, the space shuttle *Atlantis* was undergoing its final preflight checks at the space port he had helped build. In an ironic but perhaps fitting tribute to his accomplishments, Petrone's obituary drew more space in the national media than what by then was an almost routine event."

AMSTERDAM BARBER WAS AFRICAN AMERICAN POLITICAL LEADER

An Amsterdam barber, Robert A. Jackson, may have been active in the Underground Railroad before the Civil War and was an African American political leader in the late 1800s.

Montgomery County historian Kelly Yacobucci Farquhar said, "It is very possible that [Jackson] had Underground Railroad connections because he was not too far away from Chandler Bartlett's shoe store that also reputedly sheltered freedom seekers. Jackson's barbershop was in an upper floor over 69 East Main Street, which would be approximately where the Riverfront Center now sits. He lived on Charles Street."

In the late 1800s, there were newspaper accounts documenting Jackson's role in political gatherings called Colored Conventions at the Montgomery County and state levels.

Researcher Christopher Philippo said Jackson was one of five men appointed at a statewide convention of black Republicans to prepare an address to voters in 1872.

In 1879, Jackson was chosen for the committee on principles and rules at the Colored Men's Montgomery County Convention in Fonda. He was named an at-large delegate to the group's state convention in Elmira, along with John James of Amsterdam and Thomas Beekman of Fonda.

VOTE FOR BLAINE

In August 1884, Jackson delivered a rousing speech in support of Republican presidential candidate James Blaine and his running mate, John Logan, at a celebration of emancipation held in Canajoharie. Other events that day included a parade, music and a reading of the Emancipation Proclamation.

The *Amsterdam Daily Democrat* reported that Jackson's speech was fluent and enthusiastic and was applauded throughout:

> *Mr. Jackson clearly and forcibly reviewed the history of his people since the war, showing the marked difference between the attitudes of the two great parties toward them.*
>
> *The Republicans, he said, had given them the treatment they deserved and had done all in their power to dignify their condition, whereas the policy of the Democrats toward them has resulted only in their detriment.*

Blaine and Logan narrowly lost the presidential election that year to New York governor Grover Cleveland and his running mate, Thomas Hendricks. Cleveland was the first Democrat to be elected president since 1856, before the Civil War. He carried New York by a margin of just over one thousand votes to clinch the election.

MASONIC TIES

In October 1884, the *Amsterdam Daily Democrat* printed an interview with Jackson, who had recently returned from a trip to Philadelphia for the national convention of what were then called the Colored Masons. A Troy newspaper reported that Jackson originally came from Troy and had joined the Masons there.

The Amsterdam paper's interview took place at Jackson's barbershop, and he reportedly "talked rapidly away as he stropped his razor."

Jackson said the convention was the largest ever because it celebrated the 100th anniversary of the creation in Boston of the first lodge of black Free Masons in America.

Jackson said, "[The convention] was marked by a grand parade in which 25 lodges were represented in a membership of 2,000, comprising delegates from Delaware, New York, New Jersey, Maryland, Mississippi, Virginia, Kentucky, Massachusetts and Ohio."

In 1886, the Amsterdam paper reported "tonsorial artist Robert Jackson" was spending Sunday with friends in Minaville.

Farquhar said, "According to my records he was married to Hannah Herod and they had at least five children. One of their daughters, Agnes, died at the age of seven in 1882 due to meningitis. Agnes, Hannah and Robert are all buried in Green Hill Cemetery, possibly along with a couple of other daughters."

Farquhar and Judith Wellman have written *Uncovering the Underground Railroad: Abolitionism and African American Life in Montgomery County, N.Y., 1820–1890*. It is available at Farquhar's office at the old courthouse in Fonda.

Jackson died on February 19, 1893, and was about sixty. He was described in his obituary as one of the best-known African Americans in the Mohawk Valley.

The *Amsterdam Daily Democrat* wrote, "He was a man of upright lift and genial nature and had many friends."

STORMING FORT FISHER IN
THE CIVIL WAR

Bruce Anderson, an African American buried in Amsterdam, fought alongside a Canajoharie white man, Zachariah C. Neahr, in a daring mission during the second battle of Fort Fisher, North Carolina, near the end of the Civil War.

Anderson was probably born in 1845 in the country of Mexico and then worked as a farmer in New York. Some believe he was born in Oswego County. He was among a small number of African Americans who enlisted in mostly white Union regiments.

Neahr, whose friends called him Z.C., was born in Palatine in 1830 but lived most of his life in Canajoharie. Neahr married Sophia Martin in 1854. He and Anderson enlisted in Company K of the 142nd New York Infantry Regiment at Schenectady.

Fort Fisher protected the port of Wilmington, North Carolina, where blockade runners brought in supplies for Confederate troops. The Union tried unsuccessfully to capture the fort in late 1864.

THE ANGEL OF DEATH

Union warships sailed to Fort Fisher on January 12, 1865. Commanded by Admiral David Dixon Porter, the Union armada shelled the fort. A landing party went ashore, but the lightly armed force was decimated by Confederate fire.

Major General Alfred Terry's soldiers approached by land. Terry commanded four regiments, including the 115th New York from Fonda and the 146th New York, whose members included Anderson and Neahr.

A surgeon with the 117th New York Infantry wrote, "Not far in advance towered the frowning Fortress…and though none saw, all knew, that above, in imperial majesty sat the Angel of Death."

A palisade, a wall made of wooden stakes, was held by Rebel sharpshooters, making the Union advance impossible. General Newton Curtis asked for volunteers with axes to move forward and chop a breach in the palisade. Privates Anderson and Neahr were among the volunteers.

Montgomery County historian Kelly Farquhar said Anderson was not one of the men who originally volunteered but stepped forward to replace a man from Gloversville who had two small children. Anderson said he had less to lose. Neahr later told a comrade, "Right there I gave up my life for my country."

The small party managed to cut an opening in the palisade that other soldiers passed through. Most of the volunteers, however, were killed. Anderson, Neahr, Alaric Chapin, George Merrill and Dewitt Hotchkiss survived.

The Confederates surrendered that night. The next day, the main powder magazine at the fort exploded, killing two hundred men on both sides. Taking the fort, however, may have helped to hasten the end of the war.

The survivors of the raid on the palisade were recommended for Congressional Medals of Honor by General Adelbert Ames after the battle, but the paperwork was lost.

A LONG WAIT

Neahr was mustered out of the army in June 1865 and returned to Canajoharie. He and his wife, Sophia, had two children. A prominent Democrat, Neahr held two government jobs—post inspector and overseer of the poor. A trustee of the Methodist Church and a Mason, he belonged to the Farrell post of the Grand Army of the Republic.

Neahr finally received his Medal of Honor after petitioning for it. A newspaper reported, "When he got the medal in 1896 not even his wife knew of his famous deed."

Neahr died from tuberculosis on July 21, 1903. The headline in the *New York Press* stated, "Consumption claims gallant hero of historic battle."

When he died, Neahr was living on Mill Street in Canajoharie and was buried at Canajoharie Falls Cemetery. His GAR post attended the funeral as a group. His death and the Fort Fisher connection received newspaper coverage in New York City, Syracuse and Rochester.

After Neahr was awarded his medal, Anderson hired a lawyer and finally received his medal in 1914, as did two other Fort Fisher men, Alaric Chapin and George Merrill. Dewitt Hotchkiss never got his medal.

Anderson had been mustered out of the military in 1865 and returned to New York after the war. Farquhar said he lived in Johnstown and was married twice, to Adelia Anderson and Julia James. He had seven children and lived in Amsterdam in his later years. He died in 1922 at St. Peter's Hospital in Albany and is buried at Green Hill Cemetery in Amsterdam.

A Montfort Point Marine

Farquhar said she is 90 percent sure that Bruce Anderson's grandson is Ambrose "Cowboy" Anderson Jr. of Gloversville, a 2012 recipient of the Congressional Gold Medal, the nation's highest civilian award.

Anderson earned his nickname playing on the streets of Gloversville as a child. He was a football star in the 1940s. He was one of the first African American marines, called the Montfort Point Marines, entering World War II in 1943. He fought in the long and ferocious battle on Iwo Jima in 1945.

Anderson told the *Times Union* that he endured brutal treatment during the war because of his race. But on the battlefields in Iwo Jima, he said, blacks and whites worked together.

AMSTERDAM MAN WAS TWENTIETH-CENTURY INDUSTRIALIST

As Amsterdam's carpet industry declined, a local man of Polish descent created a multimillion-dollar company that manufactured furniture repair products. Frank D. Pabis started Mohawk Finishing Products with an initial investment of $5,000 in 1948.

As a child, Frank Pabis lived near Hagaman but moved when his father, Lawrence Pabis, bought a farm on Route 30 north of Amsterdam, adjacent to the site of what became the Mohawk Finishing Products factory. Frank picked potatoes on the farm as a boy and, as a teenager, worked in a local furniture store. He found that furniture often arrived scratched and dented at the store and that existing touch-up products were inferior. Pabis took chemistry correspondence courses and learned furniture repair from Joe Wartinger, an Amsterdam upholsterer who was a native of Germany.

Pabis started concocting furniture repair liquids and touch-up sticks in a barn next to the family home on Route 30, but his research was interrupted by service in the U.S. Army during World War II. After the war, he worked for a furniture repair company in Syracuse, but the owner refused to let the Amsterdam man buy into the business.

In 1948, Pabis returned to Amsterdam and established his own company in an old house on John Street in the East End. He not only devised formulas for numerous sprays, daubs and waxes to fix furniture imperfections but also designed machinery to make these products. His brothers, Edward and Steven, worked in the business. They would prepare a new product, go to

Frank D. Pabis founded a multimillion-dollar company in Amsterdam that made furniture repair products. *Walter Elwood Museum.*

furniture stores and factories to demonstrate the product and then return to fill the orders.

The business grew, and Pabis relocated to 175 West Main Street. Bob Sauval of Amsterdam went to work for Pabis in 1959, when the factory was on West Main Street and stayed with the company for thirty-eight years, eventually becoming building foreman.

Sauval said that Pabis was "a compassionate man" who "wanted to know about your family." Pabis once loaned Sauval money to tide him over a rough patch and deducted modest payments from Sauval's paycheck until the loan was repaid.

The company was called Mohawk Furniture Finishing Products. It became Mohawk Finishing Products, Inc., in 1964, the same year a large one-story plant was built on Route 30 near the family farm. Pabis and his wife, Dorothy, apparently had separated by 1970.

Mohawk Finishing was a "good place to work," according to Jen Polinski of Fort Johnson, who worked there for twenty years. Jen's husband, Ed Polinski, got a job at Mohawk Finishing first, and Jen secured employment there a few years later. In 1973, Ed Polinski was a dairy farmer, but at age fifty, he found farming difficult and hired labor hard to come by. Polinski explained his plight to Pabis, a longtime friend. Polinski said, "Frank told me, 'You sell the cows, come to me and I'll give you a job.'"

In the 1970s, the *Recorder* reported that some of the machines designed by Pabis were collected by a longtime officer of the firm, the late realtor D. Paul Wojcicki, and stored on a farm near the Route 30 factory. The collection was called "Mohawk's Smithsonian Institute."

Chester Drzewicki, who was general manager of the Amsterdam plant in the 1970s, said that Pabis was "an ingenious man, who had an inquisitive mind and determined attitude."

Mohawk Finishing Products offered classes for furniture stores and manufacturers in use of the company's repair compounds. One product was Lacover, said to repair damaged furniture without showing that a repair had been made. Another bestseller was a furniture repair kit that included fifty jars of blended stains, forty-eight repair sticks, abrasive paper, a sable brush and an electric knife.

In 1973, the firm merged with Republic Powdered Metals (RPM) of Medina, Ohio. Pabis told the *Recorder* that his two sons were not interested in taking over the family business.

Pabis was president of the Amsterdam Culture and Civic Association that sponsored the city's Polka Fest. Proud of his Polish heritage, he sold some of his products in Poland. He served on the boards of the YMCA, Housing Authority, Community Chest and Antlers Country Club. A 1978 profile described Pabis as "an energetic, bouncy man" with "silver hair and black rim glasses" who had a houseboat on Sacandaga Lake and who enjoyed fishing and golf.

Pabis headed several reelection campaigns for popular congressman Samuel Stratton. Stratton called Pabis an "outstanding businessman and industrialist" when Pabis received the annual Industry Week Award from the Amsterdam Area Chamber of Commerce in 1980, the year he retired from Mohawk Finishing. At that time, Mohawk Finishing boasted millions of dollars in yearly revenue and 200 employees, 140 of them in Amsterdam. Five months after retiring, Pabis died at age sixty-six in March 1981. He was buried at Fairview Cemetery.

The factory he began remained in Amsterdam until June 2001. The parent company, RPM, closed the Amsterdam plant then and moved Mohawk Finishing to Hudson, North Carolina. In 2005, the factory building on Route 30 in the town of Amsterdam became the home of wooden pallet manufacturer Power Pallet, according to town supervisor Thomas DiMezza.

LOUIE ALLEN'S SHRINE TO POCKET BILLIARDS

Amsterdam men who were young in the mid-twentieth century pay tribute to Market Street pool hall proprietor Louie Allen.

Richard Ellers, a 1945 Amsterdam high school graduate, said he has fond memories of Louie as a no-nonsense Dutch uncle: "We called him Reverend, partly because he was strict about behavior."

Ellers added that no cussing was allowed at Louie's, "But he was always ready to shake 'buck dice' for money or just for a soda pop and his back room was a haunt of poker players and some crap shooting."

James Romanowski, who played pool at Louie's in the 1960s, said Allen could not use his left arm, apparently a birth defect, and that Allen wore a lift in his left shoe.

Romanowski said Allen sat in the corner looking out the window of the pool hall and when a good-looking woman passed by he would say, "Yippie Skippy built for speed and comfort." An offended woman once came into the pool hall and struck Allen, or so the story goes.

Allen had a pool-playing protégé named Jimmy Corrigan. Corrigan went into the navy and died in a car crash while still a young man.

Allen's first-floor pool hall was on Market Street at an alley that led to the police station. The building was torn down for urban renewal in the 1970s, and the pool hall closed.

Romanowski had joined the marines and, when he returned to the area, sought out Allen at the former pool hall owner's camp at Great Sacandaga

Lake. Romanowski asked if he could buy any of the pool tables that had been in the establishment. Allen replied that he took the tables himself and used the slate for the patio they were standing on.

FRANK'S

When he was fifteen, Amsterdam native Mark Copp was "a heckuva pool player" at Frank's Pool Hall, above the Sears store next to the bus station on East Main Street. Copp said, "The smoke was so thick that you could hardly see the table next to you. You could buy cigarettes for two cents each [three for a nickel] from a shot glass kept under the counter."

Frank was Frank Wyszomirski. The pool hall attracted young men from the nearby Catholic high school, St. Mary's Institute, during their lunch hour.

Michael Cuddy recalled the day the principal at St. Mary's, Mother Grace, raided Frank's. As Mother Grace came up the front stairs, boys ran down the back stairs or crowded into the men's room. It was rumored that Mother Grace sometimes stationed herself with binoculars at Lurie's Department Store across the street to observe the comings and goings at Frank's.

The late John Szkaradek said of Frank's:

> There were ten tables, numbered one to ten. The first three tables were kind of for amateurs with a lot of slam bang going on. The second set of tables was better cared for. The third set of tables was very well cared for, right in front of the counter where Frank could keep a sharp eye on the play and the players. These tables were mostly used for straight pool and tournament play. Table 10 was an extra long table located at the back of the hall along with the only billiard table in the city.
>
> Billiards was something special whether you played straight billiards or three cushion billiards. There you learned about English on the ball and the use of the diamonds on the table. There was a tournament held [at Frank's] with a guest appearance of a pro named Joe Canton from Massachusetts who played the city champ, Elmer Holubetz.

The Sloth

A famous pool player named Frank Taberski lived most of his life in Schenectady but was born in 1889 in Amsterdam. According to an online source, Taberski began shooting pool in Amsterdam when he was only thirteen. Taberski turned professional in 1915 and became world champion a year later.

Taberski was nicknamed "the Sloth" and "the Inexorable Snail" because he took so long between shots. He forfeited his title in 1919 after officials set a time limit on shots. He won four more titles in the late 1920s

Taberski later owned a bowling alley and pool hall at 135 Broadway in downtown Schenectady. He died in 1941 at age fifty-two.

In 1963, at the dawn of the age when pool was becoming more upscale and family friendly, *Daily Gazette* columnist Larry Hart did a story on the traditions of pool hall culture

Taberski's former Broadway establishment was operated in 1963 by another Amsterdam native and excellent pool player, James Chiara.

Chiara told Hart that many pool players die young: "There's a lot of tension which builds up during big matches and it stays inside even after the match is over."

Chiara's nephew, Michael Chiara of Amsterdam, said his late uncle's Schenectady establishment was torn down for the Schenectady downtown parking garage.

James Chiara used to come home to Amsterdam and put on intricate trick shot demonstrations at the local pool halls. "It is a science," Michael Chiara said.

Family Friendly

Joseph Inglese of the town of Florida has memories of Dee's Billiard Lounge on Route 30 at Maple Avenue Extension in the town of Amsterdam.

Inglese said:

My good friend the late Tony DaBiere of Tribes Hill owned that establishment. In earlier years, he had a small grocery store there. Tony knew the benefits of promoting billiards as a family activity.

LOST MOHAWK VALLEY

I sat with him on many a Friday night while folks brought their youngsters in to enjoy a session of pool in the well-lit establishment.

Today the tradition of downtown pool halls is maintained by the upscale Sharp Shooters Billiards and Sports Pub on Amsterdam's East Main Street, about halfway between the old locations of Louie Allen and Frank Wyszomirski.

BALLPLAYER GEORGE BURNS
LIVED IN GLOVERSVILLE

Fulton County sports enthusiast Mike Hauser has a personal stake in advocating National Baseball Hall of Fame status for George Joseph Burns, who played his best years with the New York Giants. Burns was the brother of Hauser's great-grandfather on his mother's side.

Born in Utica in 1889, Burns lived in Little Falls and St. Johnsville before the family moved to Gloversville, where they operated a Main Street pool hall.

In 1910, Burns was in Utica watching the minor-league Utica Harps. The Harps' catcher didn't show up. According to baseball historian Richard Puff, "Bus" Nicholson, a Utica alderman who knew Burns, suggested he be hired for the game. Burns agreed to play and did well.

From there, he was hired by the New York Giants and sat on the bench most of the 1911 season to absorb the wisdom of manager John McGraw. Because of his speed and strong throwing arm, McGraw assigned Burns to left field for the Giants in 1912.

Left field at the Polo Grounds became known as Burnsville. When he retired, his total of 1,844 games in the outfield ranked sixth in National League history. He stole home twenty-one times in his career, still a league record. Burns was one of the first baseball players to use sunglasses and wear a long-billed cap.

Puff wrote in a 1983 article, "Burns was also tagged with the moniker of Silent George by his teammates and New York sports writers. Well-behaved and soft spoken, Burns was never ejected from a game in his career."

Burns led the league in runs scored in four seasons. He played in three World Series and in 1921 had a key role in game five. It was Babe Ruth's first World Series as a New York Yankee, and Ruth hit his only home run of the series in that game. But Burns hit a base-clearing double that won the game to trump Ruth's home run.

Two months later, Burns was traded to the Cincinnati Reds. Hauser has a series of letters between Burns and the Reds that give an idea of major-league salaries then. Cincinnati was offering $10,000 a year, but Burns was holding out for $12,500.

Burns remained popular with the Giants, and the team postponed its World Series celebration at the Polo Grounds until the first time Cincinnati visited for the season. Burns led the parade to center field.

Burns returned to Gloversville with the Cincinnati Reds in 1923, playing a game against the local Elks team at Parkhurst Field.

In 1924, Cincinnati traded Burns to Philadelphia, where he played for the legendary Connie Mack. Mack thought highly of Burns, according to Hauser, who quotes family sources as saying Mack would seek Burns out at ceremonies in Cooperstown even if the room included a bevy of more famous baseball stars.

Burns's major-league playing career ended in 1925, and from 1926 to 1930, he was a player-manager with minor-league teams in Texas and Williamsport, Pennsylvania.

In 1930, he returned to Gloversville to work at the family pool hall. In 1937, he went back to the New York Giants for one season as a bench coach. He returned to Gloversville the next year and worked for Levor Tanneries as a payroll clerk from 1938 until his retirement in 1957.

Burns was married twice. His first wife died. They did not have children. His second wife, Pauline, had children of her own. In later years, Burns spent time as an umpire and impressed younger players with his speed. Burns died in 1966 at age seventy-six and is buried at Johnstown's Mount Carmel Cemetery off Route 29.

There are brief black-and-white film clips showing Burns in action in the 1917 World Series playing for the New York Giants. The footage of Burns was among a cache of five hundred films discovered underground in Dawson City, Yukon, Canada. The newsreels, dated from 1910 to 1929, had accumulated in remote Dawson City when the town was the last stop on a supply chain for movies and newsreels. In 1929, the films were buried as fill underneath an ice rink and were discovered in 1978, when a new recreation center was being constructed. The films were well preserved because the objects were buried in the cold Canadian ground. Using the restored images, filmmaker Bill Morrison of New York City has created a documentary called *Dawson City: Frozen Time*.

FULTON COUNTY HALL OF FAME

In the summer of 2015, Burns was inducted into the Fulton County Baseball and Sports Hall of Fame. The Hall of Fame was founded in 2012 in coordination with the Fulton County Museum and the Fulton-Montgomery Sports Historical Society to recognize the achievements of local athletes who played at a national level or excelled in collegiate sports.

Previous inductees include Chuck Harmon, who played minor-league ball in 1947 with the Johnstown-Gloversville Glovers of the Canadian American league and then became the first African American player with the Cincinnati Reds. Jumpin' Jack Johnston, a Gloversville native, was a freestyle skier and three-time aerial freestyle world champion. Pitcher Jack Chesbro played with the Johnstown Buckskins in 1895 and went on to be the first pitcher to win a game for the New York Yankees. The team previously had been called the New York Highlanders.

Gloversville's George Joseph Burns the outfielder is sometimes confused with George Henry Burns, a first baseman who was born in 1893 in Ohio and who played in the American League. Once in a great while, the ball-playing Burnses are confused with George Burns the comedian.

BASEBALL PIONEER NICHOLAS YOUNG AN AMSTERDAM NATIVE

Nicholas Ephraim Young, one of the founders of baseball's National League, was a native of Amsterdam. Young was born in 1840, the son of Almarin and Mary Young. When he was eight years old, Young's family moved to Old Fort Johnson, the former home of colonial period Indian agent Sir William Johnson.

Young attended school in Amsterdam and played a ballgame he called "one or two old cat" in which the score was kept by notching each score on a stick.

He developed an interest in cricket, which he said had been brought to Amsterdam by English immigrants hired by the growing carpet industry.

Young recalled in a memoir at the National Baseball Hall of Fame, "The English weavers who were employed in our factories, introduced the English game of cricket and we young Americans took up their game to the exclusion of our former games, and in a very few years we had become, by constant practice, so proficient that we could beat them at their own game."

The Youngs were well off, and cricket was considered a game for the gentry. His father was of Dutch descent and operated a gristmill and grain business in Fort Johnson. Newspaper accounts described the fine meals that followed cricket matches.

Although small in stature (his military papers are marked "5 feet 6 inches" and gray eyes), Young was a nimble player. During his teen years, he competed against Canadian cricketers in this country and in Canada. In 1858, he was selected to play with the New York State cricket team against the New York City team in their annual match on a cricket field between Albany and Troy.

Young probably went to Albany to help his father's business at the age of eighteen, the year his mother died. His father was appointed Amsterdam postmaster by President Lincoln in 1861.

CIVIL WAR

According to his *New York Times* obituary, Young enlisted in the Thirty-second New York Infantry in 1862 and with that regiment, and later with the United States Signal Corps, engaged in many battles until the end of the Civil War.

Historian Robert Going wrote that Young and John Dwyer of Amsterdam, a plumber who was born in Ireland, took part in an early version of the new sport of baseball while in the Union army.

During a lull in the fighting, Dwyer was the catcher and Young the pitcher on a pioneer ball team they organized called the New Yorks. The New Yorks played a game against non–New Yorkers who called themselves the United States as a reported fifteen thousand people watched.

Young wrote in a memoir, "On our trip to Gettysburg [in 1863], we halted at a little place called Tarrytown, and as we were ordered to pitch our tents we expected to remain a few days, in which event we had arranged to celebrate the glorious Fourth of July by having a baseball match. But the next morning our bright hopes vanished as we were ordered to move on for Gettysburg,"

When the war ended, Dwyer went back to Amsterdam and was elected mayor. After the war, Young worked for the U.S. Treasury Department but continued to be active in sports.

By then, the new American game of baseball was off and running. Young was a right fielder and official of an amateur baseball team in Washington, D.C., the Olympic Club.

PLANTING AN ACORN

In 1871, Young issued a call for the first meeting of professional baseball clubs. The meeting was held in New York City, and the National Association was formed with Young as its secretary.

Nicholas Young, an Amsterdam native, was one of the founders of baseball's National League. *National Baseball Hall of Fame.*

Young later said, "From the seemingly little acorn we planted that night on St. Patrick's Day, 1871, what a giant oak has grown, spreading its branches over this greatest of all lands, and furnishing clean, honest, healthful amusement for millions of people."

Young and Mary E. Cross of Washington married in 1872. They had three sons and one daughter. In 1876, baseball's National Association became the National League, and Young continued as secretary. He also managed the Washington team and was an umpire. In 1881, he was elected president of the National League and served until 1903.

Although he was called Uncle Nick and was a popular figure, Young's term as league president was marked by conflicts. There were rowdy and violent incidents on the playing fields in the 1890s.

Harvard president Charles Eliot explained why he was considering dropping baseball as a collegiate sport, "Well, this year I'm told the team did well because one pitcher had a fine curved ball. I understand that a curve ball is thrown with a deliberate attempt to deceive. Surely that is not an ability we should want to foster at Harvard."

Many star players and top umpires went to the rival American League when it was formed in 1901. The turmoil led to Young withdrawing from consideration for a further term as president in 1903.

After his baseball career, Young returned to the Treasury Department. He died in 1916 at age seventy-six at the home of one of his sons in Washington.

Walter C. Barnes of the *Boston Globe* wrote in 1937, "No person ever connected with baseball did more for making the game what it is today than Nick Young."

IF YOU KNEW SUSIE

Angelo Sardonia was born in 1911 in Poultney, Vermont, and moved to Amsterdam as a young boy. His nickname was "Susie." It's not clear why. Some speculate he once had a crush on a girl named Susie. Since Sardonia was musical, perhaps he was a fan of the song made popular by Eddie Cantor, "If You Knew Susie."

Sardonia's daughter Maryann Salm said the nickname could have come after her father formed his band in the 1930s, Susie's Washboard Band, also known as Susie's Swingsters. The other band members were Joe Iannotti, Dennis "Junior" Hasenfuss and Jim "Dale" Dallesandro.

In his history book *Past and Present*, Tony Pacelli said the Swingsters dressed as hillbillies and made sweet music the hard way: "The instruments consisted of a guitar, a stovepipe with a kazoo on the end and a washboard with attached novelties such as whistles, horns and a toy trombone with a kazoo attached to it. The group was similar to the Spike Jones Band."

Susie's Washboard Band was a hit at the 1930 Sportsmen's Show in Amsterdam and at Leggiero's gas station on Bridge Street on the South Side, where the band drummed up business on Wednesday nights.

The Swingsters got out-of-town gigs, including the Schine Theatre in Ilion. Pacelli said the Schine Theatre chain, based in Gloversville, wanted the band to perform at all its theaters in New York, but the deal never was finalized. The musical group disbanded in the 1940s.

Sardonia worked at Chalmers Knitting Mill and its successor Montco, heading the knitting room, the dye house and maintenance.

He also owned a tavern named Susie's on Bridge Street across from the Chalmers mill. He was married to Helen Reichel, and they had a son and two daughters.

SOUTH SIDE SERVICE MEN'S NEWS

In World War II, Sardonia edited the *South Side Service Men's News* to keep soldiers far away up to date on local happenings. Members of his Fifth Ward Service Flag Committee wrote thirty-one chatty newsletters over three years.

Salm said, "Dad was never drafted. I think the *Service Men's News* was a way he could help. That little newspaper was quite an undertaking. Funding alone was a project. It took contributions and social functions to raise money. The *Recorder* and its staff were also a great help to my dad."

Salm said the newsletters were funny and sad: "It was as though you met someone on the street you knew and stopped to talk."

Amsterdam native Joseph Inglese found copies of the newsletters in old papers belonging to his grandmother. A 1945 edition eulogized the pastor of Mount Carmel Church, Reverend John Reidy, who died on February 16, 1945. Father Reidy was remembered for his judgment and advice during his sixteen years as pastor. He also was a Brooklyn Dodgers fan.

The *News* reported that Tony Fabozzi broke his shinbone in the final minutes of a basketball game between St. Mary's and Amsterdam High School. Tony had scored nineteen points when injured, and St. Mary's won the game, which was the talk of the town for days. The editor commended sportsmanship shown on both sides.

In the Men's Bowling League, the Leggiero team was tied with the Columbians. Armory Grill was only four games out, and the Altieri team had won twenty of twenty-four matches. The editor wouldn't bet a "second handed apple" on who will win. Ernie Leggiero, Shep Romano and Nick Caputo (described as "the great giant of Ballston") were leading in individual scores. In other sports, the *News* reported that the runways were being cleared for South Side bocce ball play.

"This department takes its hat off to Sgt. Al Peters who recently returned from the South Pacific and who donated a pint and a half of blood for Mrs. [Tony] Alexander," wrote the *News* about a woman who had an operation at St. Mary's Hospital. "Hurrah for our boys who are doing so much to bring comfort to anyone who is in need regardless of race, color or creed."

The Mohawk River had given up its ice pack, and the fear of flooding was past: "Our sympathy to the Public Works Department, who soon will be ridding the streets of the cinders spread on during the severe freezing weather."

Louis Martuscello and William Meyers of the army and Earl Billington of the marines had received honorable medical discharges and returned home. There were twenty South Side soldiers home on leave. Six men had left for basic training. The Fifth Ward Memorial Fund had passed $5,000.

Private Phil Marone was convalescing at Fort Ord, California, from a recent ailment and asked for letters from home. The *News* wrote, "Boy what vitamins mail contains. Here goes, Phil, for a hundred letters a day."

Another item read, "Harold Sweet [the ice man] was still traveling with 1944 truck plates when apprehended by the State Police. His only comment, 'Sorry, officer, I have new ones but I have been so busy delivering ice to war workers that I haven't had time to put them on yet.' P.S.—No fine. Case dismissed."

The war in a way had come to Sardonia's home on October 13, 1943. That night, a twin-engine army transport plane crashed in a rural section of Amsterdam's South Side as the plane's four-man crew parachuted to safety. Remarkably, there were no injuries. The plane was on a flight between Rome, New York, and Schenectady when its engines went out.

Captain John F. Pope, the last to exit the plane, was found wandering on Dewitt Street. He apparently had landed on the roof of Sardonia's house or on the nearby porch of Charles Frohlich. Accounts differ. After the war, Sardonia was instrumental in building the Fifth Ward Memorial Park on Bridge Street.

Public Service

Sardonia served over nineteen years as Fifth Ward alderman, from 1944 to 1948 and then from 1958 to 1973, when he lost an election to Lawrence Morini. Longtime friend Bert DeRose recalled that in one campaign, Sardonia organized a Kettle Band, young people banging on tin cans and buckets drumming up votes for Sardonia.

Sardonia's nephew Michael Chiara was impressed that his uncle always stood when he spoke at common council meetings while most members stayed seated during their speeches.

LOST MOHAWK VALLEY

After thirty-six years of marriage, Helen Reichel Sardonia died on December 24, 1968. In 1972, Sardonia married Margaret Schultz, a widow with two grown children, a daughter and son. Angelo Sardonia died at age seventy-six on July 3, 1987.

Sardonia's great-granddaughter Theresa Day said she named her eldest child Angela in his memory: "The stories he would tell me as I sat on his lap, I can barely remember them now, wishing I paid more attention. He was so kind and loving, gentle soul. I can remember the day he died. I was only four or so, hearing on the radio someone talking about it, me unknowing at the time, big news in Amsterdam. I really miss that man."

THE MAN WITH THE ELABORATE SIGNATURE

Francis E. Spinner, the U.S. treasurer who developed an elaborate signature to prevent counterfeiting of currency, spent time in his youth apprenticed to saddle and harness maker David DeForest in the Amsterdam area.

Spinner was born in German Flats in the western Mohawk Valley in 1802, the eldest of nine children. His father, Reverend John Spinner, was a German Roman Catholic priest who had become a Protestant and married Magdalene Brument. The Spinners came to the United States in 1801. John Spinner was pastor of two German-speaking Dutch Reformed churches in Herkimer and German Flats.

In a 1937 history, Reverend W.N.P. Dailey wrote of Spinner's youth, "A week after the child was born the house burned and the mother, barefooted, carried her infant through the snow to a neighbor's. As a lad he showed great taste for books but his father insisted on his learning a trade."

Spinner first was apprenticed to a confectioner in Albany. His father moved him to the Amsterdam area when he found out the young man was not learning how to make confections but was serving as a salesman and bookkeeper in Albany.

Spinner became an apprentice at DeForest's saddle shop on the south side of the Mohawk River in the 1820s. He showed his love of books by reading every volume in the Union Library, the first organized book collection in Amsterdam.

According to a local newspaper, Spinner had a close call when the first Amsterdam Mohawk River bridge was under construction in 1821. He was climbing along an unfinished part of the structure when it began to give way. Spinner jumped to safety as part of the bridge collapsed.

In 1824, Spinner returned to Herkimer County, where he married Caroline Caswell of Herkimer and rose to prominence as a banker. He also was a major general in the state militia and sheriff of Herkimer County. He was one of the commissioners responsible for construction of the state asylum for the mentally ill in Utica.

Francis E. Spinner as a member of Congress. Later, as U.S. treasurer, Spinner used his elaborate signature to foil counterfeiters and is remembered for hiring women for government jobs. *Library of Congress.*

A Republican, he served in Congress from 1855 to 1861. President Abraham Lincoln named Spinner the U.S. treasurer following a recommendation from Secretary of the Treasury Salmon P. Chase.

During the Civil War, Spinner recommended that women be hired as clerks because many men had become soldiers. Despite some opposition, he was able to hire one hundred women and kept them on the payroll after the war ended.

Spinner's elaborate signature became the best-known handwriting in America. He told a magazine writer that he consciously developed his signature while he was sheriff, asylum commissioner and banker.

In 1875, he resigned as U.S. treasurer in a dispute with a new secretary of the treasury who would not give Spinner final say over who would serve on his staff. That same year, Spinner ran unsuccessfully for New York state comptroller. He relocated to Jacksonville, Florida, and died in 1890. He is buried in the Mohawk Cemetery in the village of Mohawk in Herkimer County.

After his death, the women he had hired to work in the Treasury Department raised $10,000 for a bronze statue of Spinner, first located at the private Corcoran Gallery of Art in Washington. In 1909, the Daughters of the American Revolution had the statue moved to Myers Park in Herkimer.

The statue has this quote from Spinner: "The fact that I was instrumental in introducing women to employment in the offices of the government gives me more real satisfaction than all the other deeds of my life."

WALTER ELWOOD AND ROBERT FROTHINGHAM

Amsterdam museum founder Walter Elwood's own collection of natural wonders was augmented in the late 1930s and 1940s by objects including an elephant's foot from the estate of world traveler, author and advertising man Robert Frothingham. Frothingham had married a woman from the Mohawk Valley, and they had a summer home near Northville in the Adirondacks.

Elwood, born in the town of Florida, was an educator and student of nature with an extensive collection of his own from his world travels. Today's museum director, Ann Peconie, and board member Robert Going said that Elwood apparently reached out to Frothingham's widow after her husband's death in 1937 to secure items from Frothingham's collection. One story is that Elwood made the pitch while attending Frothingham's funeral. Elwood opened his Amsterdam Public School Museum at the then Fifth Ward Elementary School in 1939.

FROTHINGHAM'S LIFE

Robert Frothingham, who may have been a nephew of Fonda journalist and minister Washington Frothingham, was born in 1865 in Galesville, Wisconsin. Another ancestor was early American author Washington Irving.

Frothingham married Minnie Yerdon from a prominent Mohawk Valley farm family in 1886, and they had four children. Minnie Frothingham was descended from the Yerdon and Hess families who settled in the valley in the early 1700s. The men of the family fought in George Washington's army in the American Revolution.

Frothingham became a newspaper telegraph operator and then a reporter for the *Brooklyn Eagle* and *New York Sun* in the 1890s. He went into advertising with *Life* and other magazines. From 1914 until his retirement in 1925, he specialized in poster advertising.

Frothingham devoted time to traveling, hunting, editing, writing and lecturing. He wrote a biography, travel books and travel articles. He selected and edited anthologies of verse for publisher Houghton Mifflin.

The Frothinghams called their summer home Topside. Now occupied by distant relatives of the Frothinghams, Topside is not far from Northville.

Frothingham died of heart disease at age seventy-two on December 7, 1937, at his winter home in San Francisco. He had arrived there a week earlier after closing Topside for the winter.

1946 TOUR

Minnie Frothingham made yearly donations of objects from her late husband's collections to Elwood's museum. In October 1946, Elwood and his assistant, Amanda Powell, conducted elementary school students on a tour of newly displayed Frothingham collection items housed at the museum at the Fifth Ward School.

The *Recorder* and then a whole generation of schoolchildren marveled at "the foot of Martin Johnson's famous elephant." Johnson was a hunter and documentary filmmaker. The museum also displayed the mounted head of Old Plowshares, a moose from New Brunswick, Canada. Other Frothingham items included a caribou from the Canadian Rockies with a forty-inch antler spread. There were pelts from an Alaskan bear, a Mexican timber wolf and a snow leopard from the Himalayas.

Also on display were Eskimo ivory and beadwork, a Navajo rug and a bottle vase and a green bowl from Mexico. The Frothingham collection included well over one thousand glass slides.

Minnie Yerdon Frothingham died at age ninety in San Francisco in 1955. Robert and Minnie Frothingham are buried at Fort Plain Cemetery.

MUSEUM ON THE MOVE

Elwood also died in 1955. The collection, by then officially called the Walter Elwood Museum, was moved from the Fifth Ward School to the vacant Guy Park Avenue School in 1967.

Peconie came on board as director when the previous director, Ann Thane, was elected mayor of Amsterdam in 2007. Another longtime director in the years the museum was on Guy Park Avenue was Mary Margaret Gage.

In 2001, a nonprofit association began operating the museum. The Amsterdam School Department continued to own the school building that housed the museum and, in 2009, sold the structure to a developer who has created an apartment complex.

The museum then moved to Guy Park Manor, a historic Colonial building along the Mohawk River/Erie Canal in Amsterdam owned by the state.

Guy Park Manor was severely damaged during flooding from Tropical Storm Irene in 2011. In 2013, the Elwood Museum relocated to 100 Church Street in former Sanford carpet mill buildings purchased from the Noteworthy Corporation.

Part V

REMEMBERING THE PAST

CONTROVERSY OVER AN IMMORAL PERFORMANCE IN OLD AMSTERDAM

Two Amsterdam clergymen had concerns and asked Mayor John Dwyer to do something about it. The Rose Hill Folly Company was planning to perform on Wednesday, November 6, 1889, at the Potter Opera House on Market Street, across the thoroughfare from the future location of the Rialto Theatre.

Reverend John McIncrow of St. Mary's Roman Catholic Church and Reverend Donald Sprague of St. Ann's Episcopal Church told the mayor the Rose Hill Company had an "immoral tendency." The clergymen also asked Dwyer to ban the "posting of indecent pictorial advertisements of shows" in the city.

Rose Hill was welcomed in other communities. In Ithaca, the *Cornell Daily Sun* reported that the show promised "a program of the most excellent order of burlesque and specialties." A Philadelphia newspaper said the skits "cleverly displayed all the beauties of the company" while giving the comedians "a chance to create laughter." Vintage Rose Hill posters on the Internet today show buxom women, more clothed than you might expect.

Historian Hugh Donlon wrote that Amsterdam's Potter Opera House flourished in the 1880s "for roller skating, fairs, carnivals, plays and concerts, for about everything but opera."

Donlon said that police sometimes shut down what local leaders thought were immoral presentations at the Market Street entertainment hall.

A Strict Disciplinarian

John Patrick McIncrow was a native of Utica and enlisted at an early age in the U.S. Army. He contracted smallpox and returned to Upstate New York. After his ordination as a priest in 1873, he was assigned to Catholic churches in Syracuse and Albany.

A bronze statue of Reverend John McIncrow, an influential early pastor of Amsterdam's St. Mary's Church, overlooks the parish cemetery in Fort Johnson. *Kathy Snyder.*

He was named the rector of St. Mary's on East Main Street in Amsterdam in 1878. The East Main Street church building had opened in 1869. Previously, Catholics had worshipped at a church on the other side of the Mohawk River.

After nine years on the job, Reverend McIncrow was named irremovable pastor. Prominent in the community—he was an original trustee of Amsterdam Savings Bank—McIncrow received extensive newspaper coverage for his outspoken sermons.

McIncrow said that men who used foul language in front of workingwomen should lose their jobs: "In our mills our virtuous Catholic girls have to listen to impure expressions and ribald jests. Should a boss or any other man in any of our mills use such language to our girls, that girl should immediately inform the Knights of Labor and get the man who so insulted her Christian modesty removed from his possession—discharged from the mill."

In 1884, McIncrow publicly criticized wealthy Catholic parishioners for making contributions to Protestant churches, even though St. Mary's had accepted donations from Protestant mill owners such as carpet maker Stephen Sanford. Newspapers reported that McIncrow did not identify the men he was criticizing from the pulpit, but they were believed to be James Shanahan, Thomas Kennedy and Theodore Yund.

Charged with bigotry and intolerance, McIncrow replied, according to the *Albany Evening Journal*, "Protestantism was a heresy and Catholicism a truth."

The *Amsterdam Democrat* quoted an unnamed parishioner as saying, "His sermons are largely composed of abuse of one person or another."

McIncrow told the *Democrat*, "The only thing in the whole matter that I dislike is the threat that Catholics are likely to be excluded from employment in the mills in town. Such action as that on the part of the proprietors would stamp them as clearly with intolerance as I am charged with it."

FOUNDED PARISH SCHOOL

McIncrow founded the parish school, St. Mary's Institute; invited the Sisters of St. Joseph of Carondelet to teach there; and built them a convent. Hundreds were attending the school when McIncrow died. It was the first Catholic school incorporated under the New York State Board of Regents.

In an 1886 sermon, the priest took parents to task: "In a country where water is plenty it must be slothfulness of the parents to send their children to school dirty. If such a child should come to the institute, it will be sent home and not admitted until it comes in proper garb."

He was an outspoken opponent of abortion, writing to his bishop, "[The doctors] are conniving at the crime of abortion which is an offense rank in the sight of heaven."

McIncrow deplored drunkenness and formed the Total Abstinence and Benevolent Society. He urged parishioners to approach tavern owners in a proper manner but added, "Drive from your neighborhoods the saloons, the cause of so many evils to our people." He founded a Young Men's Catholic Club.

McIncrow had a stern message for parishioners in August 1886, according to a newspaper account:

> In alluding to the Spinners' Picnic, Father McIncrow asked his congregation to pray for such of its members as had had any connection with the festivities of the day before. A great number of sins were committed at the picnic, and a heavy responsibility rested upon the souls of those members of St. Mary's Church who gave their countenance and support to the affair.

The parish was predominately Irish American and English speaking, but confessions were heard in Italian, Spanish, Latin, French, German and Hungarian.

THE ROSE HILL FOLLY COMPANY DECISION

Mayor John Dwyer, who had to decide what to do about the clergymen's call for cancelation of the Rose Hill show, was born in Ireland and became a plumber after moving to Amsterdam by way of Quebec. He served in the Civil War with Nicholas Young, an Amsterdam man who went on to become the head of baseball's National League, the subject of another chapter in this book. Dwyer came back to Amsterdam after the war and was elected mayor in 1888. He was part of Father McIncrow's congregation.

According to the *Saratogian* newspaper, Dwyer found that the Potter Opera House's city license had expired. The mayor refused to renew it. The common council could have overruled the mayor, but the council didn't meet until the night of the show.

The *Saratogian* wrote, "The chances that the bald-headed gentlemen of Amsterdam will view the Parisian revels of the company are exceedingly slim." The Rose Hill Folly Company failed to appear that night in old Amsterdam.

After serving as Amsterdam mayor, John Dwyer was elected to the state assembly. His son, Matthew Dwyer, was the first graduate of St. Mary's Institute and became a prominent local attorney.

SUDDEN DEATH

Reverend McIncrow died suddenly of a heart attack at age forty-nine, seven years after the controversy over the Rose Hill Folly Company and just two months after he had married the couple who would become Ed Sullivan's parents.

The *Recorder* wrote, "Ten minutes before his death [at 1:15 a.m.] Father McIncrow was apparently as well as he ever was in his life."

People gathered about the church and parochial residence when day broke, and a huge crowd attended the funeral. The *Recorder* wrote, "Father was virile, able, intellectual and forcible, a strict disciplinarian, an authority in the church and community and his life has been well spent. At St. Mary's he was a power for the good, strengthening and drawing together the several thousand members of the parish."

In 1891, St. Mary's had acquired land in what is now Fort Johnson, just west of Amsterdam on Route 5, for a new parish cemetery. Father McIncrow was buried at the cemetery, and the congregation commissioned a large bronze statue of him. The sculptor was Lee Oscar Lawrie, and the McIncrow statue is inscribed with the words "Lawrie '97." Lawrie became a well-known American sculptor; he died in 1963.

The full-length statue of Father McIncrow standing in priestly robes and holding a book with a cross on it, was installed in 1902. A bronze base piece indicates that the statue was cast by Henry Bonnard Bronze Company Founders in New York City in 1898. Edouard Henri and Pierre Bonnard started their bronze works in 1872. They also did work for sculptor Frederic Remington from 1895 to 1900. Remington created the statue *Broncho Buster* with original castings in both the Oval Office of the White House and the Gloversville Public Library.

An account of McIncrow's life is part of Jacqueline Daly Murphy's book *St. Mary's Parish: A History*. The priest donated the marble altars at St. Mary's. The side altars are dedicated to his parents, Maria and William McIncrow. The high altar is dedicated to God for McIncrow's ordination into the priesthood.

The *Recorder* wrote, "He was of a jovial disposition, a warm friend, an entertaining conversationalist and pleasing companion, a connoisseur of jests and stories and a most agreeable host. He was a successful financier, capably handling the large interests of the church as well as looking out for the welfare of his parishioners."

FORT PLAIN STILL BENEFITS FROM INVENTOR WILLIAM YERDON

A man who invented a hose coupler used by America's railroads and automakers spent most of his life in Fort Plain. A foundation named for the inventor and his wife continues to support local charitable organizations.

William Yerdon was born in the town of Minden hamlet of Freysbush in 1843. He was a clerk at a grocery in Charleston Four Corners but wanted to improve himself through education.

Yerdon's father, Andrew, let William sell a colt owned by the family. Young Yerdon got fifty dollars for the colt and used the money to pay for tuition at the educational seminary in Fort Plain, which later became the Clinton Liberal Institute. Yerdon worked after hours for his meals.

He left Fort Plain for a time, doing hotel work in Fayetteville near Syracuse. Upon his return to Fort Plain, he was a clerk at the Clark & Woods store.

Yerdon married Sylvina Barker in 1881, according to an account in the *Mohawk Valley Register* newspaper. In later years, "Sylvina" was shortened to "Vina."

Historian Nelson Greene wrote that Yerdon took over a horse-drawn bus line and baggage transfer service. The Fort Plain bridge over the Mohawk River washed out, and Yerdon replaced the span with his own toll bridge, making a substantial profit.

A staunch Republican, Yerdon belonged to a local political organization called the Big Four. He was named postmaster in 1889, succeeding David Hackner, at the start of the presidential administration of Republican

Benjamin Harrison. Amsterdam congressman John Sanford recommended Yerdon for the post.

"The appointment of William Yerdon as postmaster at Fort Plain, under the circumstances, will be in strict accord with the sentiment of boodle as exemplified by the Republican Party in the late campaign," wrote the *Amsterdam Morning Sentinel*, a Democratic newspaper. "It is stated that Congressman Sanford has endorsed Yerdon, who virtually bought the resignation of the Democratic incumbent. This is one of those cases where President Harrison would be justified in exercising his high prerogative independent of the recommendation of a congressman, and we are surprised to know that Neighbor Sanford has voluntarily become a party to a trick so palpably wicked. Yerdon ought to get left." Yerdon served as postmaster for five years.

In 1890, Yerdon patented an invention called the Yerdon Double Hose Band. The band was an adjustable metal clamp that could securely join two sections of hose. Railroads, including the West Shore and New York Central locally, used the product.

In 1893, the *Mohawk Valley Register* announced that Yerdon was building a new factory in Fort Plain to make the hose bands. The newspaper reported he also had invented Yerdon's Perfected Can Opener. Late in life, Yerdon added the Elwood Coal Company to his business activities.

The inventor, businessman and former postmaster died in 1911 at age sixty-three after a two-year illness. He lived on River Street. He left his widow; a son, Leland; and a daughter, Lucille. He was a trustee of the Universalist Church and member of the Fort Plain Club.

Historian Greene wrote in 1925 that Yerdon's heirs continued manufacturing the hose bands after his death and found new customers in the automobile industry: "They manufacture these bands in all sizes from those no larger than a man's finger to bands four feet in diameter." There was no word on what happened to the can opener invention.

Leland Yerdon was a captain in the U.S. Army in World War I and served as chief cook in the U.S. Merchant Marine in World War II. He married Beatrice Green and lived in Fort Plain. When he died at age sixty-five in 1954, his obituary stated that the Yerdon Hose Band Company was no longer in existence.

The Yerdons' daughter, Lucille, lived in Fort Plain until shortly before her death on July 13, 1973. She attended Vassar College, never married and may have been a schoolteacher. She lived in the family home on River Street until two months before her death, when she entered the Canajoharie Nursing Home.

Her will provided numerous donations to institutions including hospitals, the then Universalist church in Fort Plain and Fort Plain Library. She donated the family home to the village, although the village board did not accept the gift, fearing the cost of maintenance would be too high.

One month after Lucille's death, the press reported her will had created the William and Vina B. Yerdon Foundation, named for her parents. According to current foundation official David Briggs and online tax records, the foundation has made monetary contributions to charitable and community organizations in the Fort Plain area ever since.

Among the donations made during 2010, for example, were $12,000 to the Fort Plain Cemetery, where the Yerdons are buried; $7,000 to Fort Plain Library; $7,000 to youth baseball in Fort Plain and $6,000 to the Ayers Animal Shelter in Sprakers. Miss Yerdon was said to have been fond of dogs and had provided in her will for the care of her own pet dog. Other organizations that have received funds from the Yerdon Foundation include the Fort Plain Museum, the senior center and village parks.

LIGHTNING TOOK THE LIFE OF FAMED FORT JOHNSON SKATER

Speed-skating champion Ted Ellenwood Jr., twenty-seven, died instantly on June 11, 1946, when struck by lightning while golfing on the Antlers Course in Fort Johnson. A friend, Lee DeGroff, was ten feet away but not injured. The golf course today is called Rolling Hills.

Ellenwood had skated for the Fort Johnson Athletic Association, which produced other top racers, including Hank Flesch, Don Talmadge and Gene Gage.

Ellenwood was an inspiration to Gage and once gave him a fine pair of skates that Gage used in racing competitions until he was in his mid-thirties. Gage is now in his mid-eighties.

Born in Dunkirk, New York, in 1919, Ellenwood and his family moved to Fort Johnson when he was five. He started skating at age ten. He won the Eastern States Speed Skating Championship in Fort Johnson in 1941. He tied for third place at the North American races in Schenectady. He won the 220- and 440-yard races at the National Championships in LaCrosse, Wisconsin, just before entering the U.S. Navy in 1942.

A machinist's mate, Ellenwood served in the war aboard the destroyer USS *Cotton*, which took part in numerous actions in the South Pacific. He; his wife, Lucia (from Portland, Maine); and their five-month-old son, Ted III, had returned to the local area to settle down by purchasing a gas station in Fort Johnson.

Fort Johnson speed skaters, circa 1940. *Left to right*: Charles Snyder, Don Ricicle, Ben Kusak, Hank Flesch, Don Talmadge, Marvin Conover, unknown, Olympic qualifier George Hare, Leroy Eckerson, Dick Snyder and Ted Ellenwood, killed in 1946 by a golf course lightning strike. *Walter Elwood Museum.*

ANOTHER CHAMPION

Ellenwood never qualified for the U.S. Olympic speed-skating teams because he was better at the American style of skating than the European style used in the Olympics. American skaters raced in a group while European skaters went in pairs and a time clock was used.

George Hare of Fort Johnson was very good at European-style racing and was named a regular on the U.S. Olympic team in 1939. Hare competed in events in the United States as an Olympian, but there were no Olympic games in 1940 and 1944 because of the war.

Among Fort Johnson skating coaches in the late 1930s and early 1940s were Leroy Eckerson and W.C. Snyder.

Fort Johnson Athletic Association speed-skating program. *Jerry Snyder.*

REMEMBERING THE PAST

POSTWAR

Another top skater for the Fort Johnson club was Raymond Knapik, who won a gold medal in the 220-yard sprint at the national speed-skating championships in Alpena, Michigan, in 1948. Knapik, who grew up in Amsterdam, also skated at Hasenfuss Field in that city.

Amsterdam native and longtime Californian Fred Wojcicki and LaVerne Colts ran the Fort Johnson skating rink in the winters of 1949 and 1950. Wojcicki for a time was president of the Northeastern Skating Association.

FORT JOHNSON MEMORIES

Fort Johnson native David Noyes, born in 1931, said when he was a child, adults in the village provided children with lifetime values by deed and example and maintained an active community.

Noyes, who lives now in Colorado, recalled commercial institutions in Fort Johnson such as Whalen's grocery store, Huen's gas station, Sweet's furniture store and Tollner's ice cream shop.

Noyes was the second of four Noyes brothers. His brother Dan drowned in the Mohawk River in 1947; his brother Randy died in an accident while serving in the U.S. Air Force. His brother Harold also lives in Colorado.

After U.S. Army service in the 1950s, David Noyes married Mary Gawron of Amsterdam and earned degrees from the SUNY College of Forestry. His career took him to the world headquarters of Johns Manville Corporation in Denver.

Describing himself as one of the "run of the mill" skaters in Fort Johnson, Noyes said he picked up a few medals along the way. He kept skating until knee and hip replacement surgeries in 2000.

DOCTOR RIGGS AND HIS STOMACH GLOBULES

The great-granddaughter of a homeopathic physician and pharmaceutical maker from Amsterdam finally has secured one of her ancestor's signature products: Dr. Riggs' Stomach Globules for Dyspepsia and Indigestion. Dyspepsia is pain in the stomach caused by difficulty digesting food.

Anne DeGroff of Amsterdam had been looking for the stomach globules for forty years and finally secured them from eBay with the help of Jerry Snyder, president of Historic Amsterdam League.

John V. Riggs was born in Schenectady in 1839. His father was publisher of a local newspaper, the *Schenectady Cabinet*. Young Riggs studied medicine at Albany Medical College and the Buffalo College of Physicians and Surgeons.

Medicine and music dominated his life. After becoming a doctor, he joined a minstrel troupe based in San Francisco as an interlocutor and bass soloist. While on tour in the South, though, he left the troupe to study yellow fever, which was widespread there.

He came back to the Mohawk Valley, opening a doctor's office at 29 Market Street in Amsterdam. He married Annie Wilds of Schenectady in 1861. He founded and directed the Arion Society, an Amsterdam singing group.

In 1889, Riggs took a chance. He sold his medical practice and went to New York City to become a professional singer. Riggs came back to

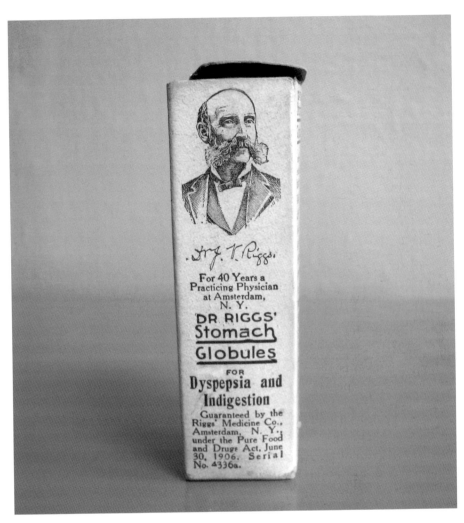

A stomach medicine manufactured in the early 1900s in Amsterdam by Dr. John Riggs, who was also a musician. *Jerry Snyder.*

Amsterdam within two years, opened a drugstore on Market Street and made a living manufacturing medicines, including the stomach globules.

A 1911 newspaper ad for the product stated:

> *Every man is a rascal as soon as he is ill. At least that was the eminent opinion of the late Dr. [Samuel] Johnson. It is well understood that a morbid and grouchy condition irritates men and women. It's my liver you say, and you diet, eat new food-stuffs, take quack remedies etc.*

Dr. John Riggs advertised that his stomach globules were little medicated pellets, easy to carry and easy to take. *Jerry Snyder.*

More likely the trouble is with the stomach: not the liver at all. Some one of the powerful fluids that aid indigestion is not performing its duties. Dr. Riggs' Stomach Globules will give you almost instant relief. Try it and you'll be surprised with the result. They're little medicated pellets, easy to carry and easy to take.

Prepared from Dr. J. V. Riggs' original formula by the Riggs' Medicine Co., in the Blood Building. At all leading drugstores. Price 50¢. Only genuine when bearing Dr. Riggs' signature.

REMEMBERING THE PAST

While marketing his potions (including Dr. Riggs' Wine of Cod Liver Oil, the great reconstructor), Riggs continued to perform as a singer. He was a member and one-time director of the St. Ann's Episcopal Church choir.

Annie Wilds Riggs died in 1909, and Dr. Riggs died on Thanksgiving eve in 1917. On Thanksgiving night, their son James S. Riggs carried on the family musical tradition. The younger Riggs conducted the Liberty Bond Vocal Club at a concert that raised $150 to make life easier for Amsterdam soldiers who had been drafted into the U.S. Army.

AMSTERDAM WAS ONCE A BOBSLED CENTER

B eing a city of hills, Amsterdam was ideal for the winter sport of bobsledding. In the late 1800s and early 1900s, winter coasting carnivals brought visitors from miles around to slide down steep city thoroughfares including Market, Northampton, Bell and Locust.

The *Amsterdam Daily Democrat* gave a full account of a nighttime coasting carnival in February 1887 on Market Street. There was a parade and parties after the races, which went on into the night. Red flares and Japanese lanterns lighted the course.

The bobsleds had front and rear steering, clanging bells and brake systems, according to historian Hugh Donlon. "Much depended on the steersmen and brakeman of the teams that ranged from ten to twenty men, all colorfully uniformed. The Joker Club, for instance, wore red St. Nicholas caps, red coats, blue cuffs and collars, blue knee breeches, red stockings and low shoes."

Despite the precautions, serious and sometimes fatal accidents resulted, and the sport was finally banned in Amsterdam in the 1920s as motor traffic increased.

For the coasting carnival on Valentine's night in 1887, the weather was not ideal. Amsterdam had a thaw, not the clear, bracing weather that was desired. Nonetheless, the newspaper reported the evening was "fairly successful."

A dozen or more coasting clubs arrived from Albany on the 6:16 p.m. train, which included a special car for their handsome bobsleds or bobs. The

REMEMBERING THE PAST

National Guard's Thirteenth Brigade Band played. The "hungry bobbers" did "ample justice" to food provided at the YMCA and Hotel Warner.

The band played again at 7:30 p.m. for a parade through downtown and up Market Street hill for a fireworks display. Albany's clubs included several named Yum Yum. Other clubs included Beverwyck, Monitor and Tammany Hall, named for the New York Democratic Party political machine.

The newspaper reported, "The bobbers presented a very pleasing appearance in their neat and tasteful uniforms. The Beverwyck club were attired in dark blue and white, the Yum Yums in orange, the Monitor club in gray, and the Tammany Hall club in plaid suits."

Clubs from Fort Plain and other points west arrived on the 8:43 p.m. train. Coasting began at 9:00 p.m., but there were no races as it was too dark.

The *Democrat* wrote, "The bob Beverwyck made the first trip down the slide. As it was turning the corner at the foot of the hill it went over the bank. The bobs Niagara, Bob Moore and Nonpareil, which were close behind, ran into the Beverwyck. The crews of the bobs were thrown into a confused mass. Several persons received injuries."

The bobs were hauled by teams of horses up Northampton Road to the top of Market Street hill for the next event. Yum Yum '88 tipped over during

Bobsledding was a popular but dangerous sport in the late 1800s and early 1900s in the hilly Mohawk Valley. This team was from Hagaman, near Amsterdam. *Hagaman Historical Society.*

the second slide down the hill. On that run, Yum Yum '87 collided with Yum Yum '86.

The wounded were taken to the house of Dr. Timmerman. One injured man spent the night at the Hotel Warner and was attended by two Amsterdam doctors.

Despite the accidents, the *Democrat* wrote, "The heavy bobs sped down the hill like lightning and the coasters greatly enjoyed the sport. The Tammany Hall was one of the fastest, if not the most fleet bob on the slide. The Flyway of Fort Plain made good time."

The Amsterdam Coasting Association entertained at a party at the YMCA after the event. The out-of-town teams left on midnight trains east and west.

Some Albanians stayed overnight and enjoyed a barouche ride the next day. A barouche is a stylish horse-drawn carriage.

BIBLIOGRAPHY

Dauria, Susan R. "Deindustrialization and the Construction of History and Ethnic Identity: The Case of Amsterdam, New York." PhD diss., University at Albany, 1999.

Donlon, Hugh P. *Annals of a Mill Town: Amsterdam, New York*. Schenectady, NY: Donlon Associates, 1980.

Douglas, Kirk. *The Ragman's Son: An Autobiography*. New York: Simon and Schuster, 1988.

Dunn, Steve, and Bob Cudmore. *Historic Views of the Carpet City: Amsterdam, N.Y.* (Documentary) WMHT-TV, 2000.

Farquhar, Kelly Yacobucci. *Images of America: Montgomery County*. Charleston, SC: Arcadia Publishing, 2004.

Farquhar, Kelly Yacobucci, and Judith Wellman. *Uncovering the Underground Railroad: Abolitionism and African American Life in Montgomery County, N.Y., 1820–1890*. Fonda, NY: Montgomery County, 2012.

Farquhar, Kelly Yacobucci, and Scott G. Haefner. *Images of America: Amsterdam*. Charleston, SC: Arcadia Publishing, 2006.

Going, Robert N. *Honor Roll: The World War II Dead of Amsterdam, N.Y.* Amsterdam, NY: George Street Press, 2010.

———. *Where Do We Find Such Men?* Amsterdam, NY: George Street Press, 2013.

Greene, Nelson. *History of the Mohawk Valley: Gateway to the West, 1614–1925*. Chicago: S.J. Clarke Publishing Co., 1925.

Hildebrandt, Louis, Jr. *Hurricana: Thoroughbred Dynasty, Amsterdam Landmark*. Troy, NY: Troy Bookmakers, 2009.

BIBLIOGRAPHY

Larner, Paul K. *Our Railroad: The History of the Fonda, Johnstown & Gloversville Railroad (1867–1893)*. Bloomington, IN: Author House, 2009.

McMartin, Barbara, and W. Alec Reid. *The Glove Cities: How a People and Their Craft Built Two Cities*. Caroga, NY: Lakeview Press, 1999.

Murphy, Jacqueline Daly. *St. Mary's Parish: A History*. Amsterdam, NY: St. Mary's Church, 2004.

Pacelli, Tony. *Past and Present: Nostalgia, Amsterdam and Surrounding Communities*. Amsterdam, NY: Recorder, 1987.

Puff, Richard A. "Silent George Burns: A Star in the Sunfield." *Research Journal of the Society for American Baseball Research* 12 (1983).

Snyder, Gerald R., and Robert von Hasseln. *Amsterdam*. Charleston, SC: Arcadia Publishing, 2010.

Tunney, Jay. *The Prizefighter and the Playwright: Gene Tunney and George Bernard Shaw*. Richmond Hill, ON: Firefly Books, 2010.

ONLINE INFORMATION

George Senator's testimony regarding President John Kennedy's assassination and Jack Ruby's killing of Lee Harvey Oswald is contained in Hearing Volume XIV of the *Warren Commission Report* published by the U.S. Government Printing Office. The testimony is online at http://jfkassassination.net/russ/testimony/senator.htm.

Tom Tryniski maintains a searchable database of many New York State newspapers: http://www.fultonhistory.com/Fulton.html.

Frank Yunker maintains a database of Bob Cudmore's *Daily Gazette* columns plus other information: www.mohawkvalleyweb.com.

INDEX

INDEX

INDEX

ABOUT THE AUTHOR

Bob Cudmore has written a weekly newspaper column on Mohawk Valley history for the *Daily Gazette* for over fifteen years. He is the author of *Stories from the Mohawk Valley* and *Hidden History of the Mohawk Valley*, published by The History Press. Cudmore also has published *You Can't Go Wrong*, a satirical book about Upstate New York.

A radio and television personality, Cudmore hosts "The Historians Podcast" online at www.bobcudmore. com/thehistorians and www. soundcloud.com (search Eastline Studio). The program also airs on RISE, WMHT's radio service for the blind and print disabled in Albany.

Cudmore did the morning show on WVTL radio in Amsterdam from 2004 to 2014. From 1980 to 1993, he hosted the nightly *Contact* talk show on WGY radio in Albany.

Bob Cudmore. *Ihor Rymaruk.*

ABOUT THE AUTHOR

A former adjunct professor in mass media at Albany's College of St. Rose, Cudmore worked in public relations for the State University of New York. He has an MA and a BA in English from Boston University.

A native of Amsterdam, he lives in Glenville with his sweetie, Audrey Sears, and has two children: Bob Cudmore Jr. of Baltimore, Maryland, and Kathleen R. Bokan of West Charlton, New York.